THE SELF-KNOWER
A HERO UNDER CONTROL

THE PLENUM SERIES IN SOCIAL/CLINICAL PSYCHOLOGY
Series Editor: C. R. Snyder

University of Kansas
Lawrence, Kansas

A Continuation Order Plan is available for this series. A continuation order will bring delivery of each new volume immediately upon publication. Volumes are billed only upon actual shipment. For further information please contact the publisher.

THE SELF-KNOWER

A HERO UNDER CONTROL

ROBERT A. WICKLUND

AND

MARTINA ECKERT

Universität Bielefeld
Bielefeld, Germany

PLENUM PRESS • NEW YORK AND LONDON

Library of Congress Cataloging-in-Publication Data

Wicklund, Robert A.
    The self-knower : a hero under control / Robert A. Wicklund and
Martina Eckert.
        p.   cm. -- (The Plenum series in social/clinical psychology)
    Includes bibliographical references and index.
    ISBN 0-306-43988-3
    1. Self-perception. 2. Social perception.   I. Eckert, Martina.
II. Title. III. Series.
BF697.5.S43W53 1992
155.2--dc20   91-44856
                                                                 CIP

ISBN 0-306-43988-3

©1992 Plenum Press, New York
A Division of Plenum Publishing Corporation
233 Spring Street, New York, N.Y. 10013

Printed in the United States of America

PREFACE

The self-knower has become a hero within many contemporary cultures. This hero goes by various different titles, including the "self-insightful," the "self-actualized," the "autonomous and mature," the "representative of independent thinking," the "morally virtuous," and many more. The common denominators of civilization's preoccupation with the self-knower are (1) the mundane, popular literature that draws our attention to our "inner being" and (2) the remarkable intensity of therapies and quasitherapies that promise insight into the true core of our inner being. A characteristic example from an extensive, week- or month-long training course would read, "Come because you want to discover your self. . . . Through Mr. X [the group leader], we can realize our true identities. . . . This gives our lives sense and perspective."

We have tried to trace the logic underlying the diverse self-knower movements and have found three common themes underlying them. For one, the varieties of theories and treatments associated with self-knowledge are interested exclusively in the *appearance* of the self-knower. Each representative of the self-knower school has its own set of criteria for identifying the self-knowing person, and in turn, each member of the self-knower school represents certain convictions about how individuals should be evaluated. For instance, if someone manifests warmth and charity, that person is likely to be pronounced healthy, adjusted, and self-knowing.

A second common theme in the self-knower movement is its distaste for looking at the social circumstances or other elements in a person's background that might underlie the self-knowing essence. Social influence, childhood training, the implanting of society's values, and the like are all regarded as irrelevant to the accumulation of self-knowledge. In fact, the presence of *any* kind of social influence is said to work against self-discovery. Instead, self-knowledge is to be achieved by shunting aside all forms of social facades (i.e., current or past social influence) and homing in on the "genuine core" of oneself.

The third common theme is a thoroughgoing confusion of *self* with *self-knowledge*. The confusion amounts to the self-knower school's not recognizing that self-aspects, such as personality traits or values, can have an existence and history quite separate from *knowledge* of those aspects. The two are commonly run together, in that it is assumed that people with certain kinds of dispositions (e.g., nonprejudiced) necessarily possess a global self-knowledge. Following this reasoning, it becomes impossible for prejudiced people to have self-knowledge, even of their own prejudice.

Elaborating on a commentary by Zurhorst (1983), our central theme is that the self-knower movement embodies a strong propensity to control individuals. The self-knower practitioner or theorist sets up criteria that are said to indicate true self-knowledge, and then individuals are said to embody healthy self-knowledge as long as they manifest these criteria. An example: If a person displays warmth, discloses a great deal, and represents a slightly left-of-center political philosophy, many of the self-knower philosophies would pronounce that person a healthy personality. Other individuals are thereby condemned to a non-self-knowing status; but if the proper education, self-experiencing training, or other therapy can shift the person's manifest values in the right direction, the person then joins the self-knowers. In short, the individual is controlled by criteria that allow—or disallow—membership among the "self-knowing" elite.

In the course of this book, we look more carefully at these processes of interpersonal control. The reader's attention is drawn to empirical work that illustrates the control mechanism underlying the self-knower movement. It is shown that the observer—the perceiver of other persons—is especially reluctant to accord the other person self-knower status, maturity, creativity, and the like, when the other is not immediately controllable.

Disentangling the heretofore highly accepted conceptions about the self-knower is just half our purpose. The other half of our perspective is a psychological analysis of self-knowledge that begins with psychological variables, not with criteria for judging whether or not persons are basically self-knowing. At least three theoretical directions in personality and social psychology have a direct bearing on self-knowledge in the sense of the person's cognizing of the self. Even though the label *self-knowledge* is not always associated with these directions, each of them offers a theoretical framework within which to treat the knowledge of one's self-components and the background of such knowledge, plus their consequences for think-ing and behaving. One of these theoretical approaches analyzes self-knowledge as a direct derivative of overt behaviors; a second treats self-knowledge as society's labeling of the person; and a third looks directly at the coming and going of self-directed attention. Accordingly, we attempt to offer the reader a basis for looking at self-knowledge within the context of causal social factors. Our modest proposal is that such systematic treat-ments can readily supplant the quasipsychology that underlies the inter-personal control problems of the self-knower movement.

Discussions and literature exchanges with Alois Angleitner were in-strumental in our undertaking this project; we thank him for his coopera-tion in talking about the issues. To C. R. Snyder we are indebted for a careful reading of the manuscript and for his interest in the book in his role as series editor. Thanks are also due to Cathaleene J. Macias for a critical reading of the entire manuscript. The production of the book owes much to the efforts of Ursula Brockmann-Lux, Ute Esselmann, Jürgen Gebauer, Heide Meise, and Katharina Schaadt. Their typing, editing, and organizing have contributed greatly to taking the rough edges off the preliminary drafts.

CONTENTS

Chapter 5

The Therapist and the Researcher: When Control Needs Determine the Ascription of Self-Knowledge

Chapter 6

Self-Knowledge: A Basis in Perception, Behavior, and Logic

Chapter 9

Self-Knowledge Viewed in a Symbiotic Relationship: The Need to Control Meets the Readiness to Be Controlled

CHAPTER 1

SELF-KNOWLEDGE

WHAT ARE WE TALKING ABOUT?

Let us try to take *self-knowledge* out of the realm of everyday parlance and ask whether it can be studied scientifically, as a psychological event. That is, does self-knowledge have causes, do certain events set it in gear, and do we know how to recognize it, measure it, and examine its consequences? How should we proceed in exploring such an all-encompassing concept— one surrounded by conventional folk wisdom and an absence of scientific underpinnings?

For a start, the reader may like to have an answer to the question, "Knowledge of what?" If we have knowledge of a self, of a being, of an identity or personality, or of other human features, how do we characterize these features? What is it that is known? This question has been skirted in most treatises on self-knowledge, and this is the place where psychology can finally show what it has to offer.

Many psychologists make reference to William James (1890) when it becomes necessary to talk about self-components. The "What is the self?" issue was handled by James in a most exacting manner. For example, he referred to a kind of visible, or observable, self, which he made equivalent to all material things (or people) associated with a person. He said that this "material" self is made up of a person's body, clothing, job, family, nation, and any other tangible entities associated with the person. Of course, the modern, critical psychologist would be skeptical about such sweeping pronouncements. How do we know, for instance, that a person's nation

1

functions as a part of the self? What does that mean psychologically? Interestingly, James had an answer: If we defend our nation's pride (or our family, or the quality of our clothing), then the nation (or other component) counts as a self-aspect.

Note that we can view the self as both a structure and a set of processes, a distinction pointed out by Snyder, Irving, Sigmon, and Holleran (1991). The Jamesian structure is composed of self-components, such as body, clothing, and opinions about oneself. The process involves actions taken in regard to that structure, such as defending those components.

James did not stop with the material self. His *social* self is constituted of others' opinions, insofar as the person is the object of those opinions. Children are aware of what their mothers, fathers, grandparents, and teachers think of them, and each of these opinions or evaluations counts as an element of the social self. James carried his point to extremes in observing that we have as many social selves as there are people who have an opinion about us.

One leap further away from the material self: James also spoke of a *spiritual* self, which consists of inner psychic qualities such as the sense of volitional decisions or the experience of emotions and desires. It is fair to say that James was less explicit about the exact nature of this facet of the self, perhaps because of its intangibility.

Self-knowledge in the Jamesian context has a very clear meaning, provided that the reader assents to James's views about the tripartite contents of the self. To know oneself would mean to know that one's body, clothing, and family are strongly associated with one's own being. It would also mean that a person can discriminate between self and nonself, in that the material world can be divided subjectively into self-components and non-self-components. Exactly how such self-knowledge is ascertained is not available in James's treatise, but for now, that does not matter. The important issue is James's answer to the question, "What self is known?" and here we see that the self is easy to recognize: It consists of material components, others' evaluations, and inner psychological mechanisms.

THE "KERNEL OF SELF" FORMULATION

Although James's tripartite self seems to cover all the possibilities in characterizing the makeup of a person's self, there is an alternative, albeit much less tangible, view. This view can be labeled the *inborn kernel of self* position. It is assumed within this school of thought that every person carries an innate self, a certain, scarcely describable essence—a vague structure—that can be discovered ever so gradually. The role of outside factors in developing or unfolding this self is nil. By definition, the self-kernel cannot be shaped by *any* outside factors whatsoever, and such elements as socializing influences are seen as merely disrupting or interfering with the workings of the innate self. This widespread view is indeed popular, as documented in critiques by Wallach and Wallach (1983) and Zurhorst (1983), and as we will see in the following chapters, it may be popular because it depicts the human as "basically and essentially good." Unfortunately, the self—the very object to be described or "known" in self-knowledge—is hardly describable within this approach. It is a vague *something,* and this school of thought assumes that people know when they have discovered this vague something.

BEHAVIORAL POTENTIAL: THE SELF OF INTEREST
TO PSYCHOLOGY

For a moment, let us leave the preceding approaches to the self aside and consider how psychologists actually go about their business. For a start, consider the vast arena of self-concept research (Wylie, 1974). Nearly all of the research and theorizing in this realm deals with self-evaluation: "How good am I?"; "How good am I in comparison with others?"; "How strong are my Characteristics X, Y, and Z relative to my ideals for those characteristics?" These self-evaluations are largely directed toward skills in social settings, a person's intellectual process, readiness to strive and achieve, and the like. A similar observation is possible when we examine relatively modern research on the self (e.g., Duval & Wicklund, 1972; Fazio & Zanna, 1981; Markus, 1983). The investigator's interest is first in a self-observation: The respondent claims to have a certain kind of behavioral potential, such as high sociability or perhaps low punitiveness, and then the actual behaviors stemming from those claims are examined under a variety of conditions. In psychological therapy, the approach is similar. The focus is on aspects of the person that underlie behavioral disturbances or inadequacies, and one would not, for instance, pay much heed to the patient's material possessions (James, 1890). Rather, the self as a source of behavior is the deciding element.

At the same time, the self that is antecedent to the behavior is not regarded as identical to the behavior. Rather, the self as a kind of behavioral potential is assumed to be a readiness, capability, latent tendency, or capacity. The reader will recognize the self as behavioral potential quite readily if we offer a few examples:

1. *Authoritarianism* (Adorno, Frenkel-Brunswik, Levinson, & Sanford, 1950) is regarded as a personality trait, as the product of childhood ex-

periences. The person possessing this personality, or behavioral potential, is said to have a tendency to think in terms of black and white, to pay heed to authority figures, and to respect social systems of hierarchies.

2. A *proecology attitude* is also a behavioral readiness or potential. People with such attitudes should be expected to respond positively to appeals to clean up the landscape or to boycott ecologically harmful products.

SELF-KNOWLEDGE OF ONE'S POTENTIAL

Psychologists who deal with such concepts as authoritarianism and proecology attitudes assume that their respondents *possess* these potentials; there is, however, no assumption that the respondents simultaneously *know* their potentials. And for the most part, research on the self is conducted without any assurance that people are consciously thinking about or reflecting on their self-components before they behave according to these components. When a researcher selects subjects with extreme political attitudes to see whether they are particularly resistant to communication, there is no assumption that each respondent is consciously attuned to that extreme attitude at the time of the communication. The research allows the *self* (in this case, the specific attitude) to run its course, to have its effects, without the subject's necessarily being attuned cognitively to the self.

The case is similar when people with certain personality characteristics are selected for study, such as highly prejudiced individuals. The researcher or observer expects that a highly sociable person (as assessed by a personality-measuring instrument) will indeed tend to show sociable behavior patterns. However, there is almost never an explicit assumption that the respondents are consciously attuned to that personality trait while behaving. In short, the question of whether self-knowledge accompanies the effects of existing attitudes or existing personality traits is seldom asked. Obviously, people can *report* their attitudes or personality characteristics when asked, but this ability says nothing about their being attuned cognitively to those self-aspects when they are behaving or prior to behaving.

Self-knowledge can thus be treated as an element that can either accompany the functioning of the self or *not* accompany that functioning. In short, self-knowledge can be regarded as a psychological variable, in that some individuals might be highly attuned to certain behaviorally relevant self-components, and other individuals would not be attuned to those same components.

"What self is to be known?" has, then, a straightforward answer when we consider the main thrust of the use of the term *self* within psychology.

Aside from whether we regard self-knowledge as something that is continuing or short-lived, whether we view it as a broad tendency or a behavior-specific knowledge, the idea is that a person's various *behavioral potentials* constitute the self that can be known. What is, then, the psychologist's task? If self-knowledge as a variable is going to be studied and implemented in practice, and if individuals are to be assessed or evaluated for their extent of self-knowledge, the psychologist needs to come to terms with such questions as:

1. What circumstances, such as training or momentarily experienced settings, bring a person to be acutely aware of certain self-dimensions?
2. What circumstances cause the awareness of certain self-dimensions to diminish or vanish?
3. How does the psychologist recognize individuals who are already cognitively attuned to their self-aspects?
4. What are the consequences of self-knowledge for further thinking processes and for behavior?

AN OUTLINE

The purpose of the chapters to follow stems directly from questions such as those listed above. These chapters attempt to look carefully at the ways in which psychology has dealt with self-knowledge. In Chapter 2, we outline in more detail how a systematic or theoretical psychology of self-knowledge can proceed. The starting point is the clear separation of *self* and *self-knowledge:* as we have seen above, the functioning of self-components can be studied quite independently of the variable self-knowledge, and it is then interesting to consider the manner in which these two separable elements—the self and knowledge of that self—can be brought together.

As history would have it, psychology has not always regarded the presence of self-aspects and knowledge of those aspects as two separate events. Rather, the majority of the theoretical and practical pronouncements on self-knowledge mix up these two. For instance, one theoretical direction claims that the presence of creativity is the signal of a self-knowing person. But within such a conception, it is not possible for creative persons to have more, or less, knowledge of their creativity. The *presence* of a trait (creativity) is mixed up with *knowledge* of the trait. Chapter 3 examines these kinds of developments and illustrates the breadth of their acceptance within the psychological literature.

Chapter 3 continues the theme of confusing contents of the self with knowledge of the self and points to the errors that result when self-knowledge is treated in this manner. For example, the mixing of the two brings problems in pointing to causes: Where do self-components stem from and where does self-knowledge come from? It seems reasonable enough that the presence of a trait (e.g., sociability) has certain origins in childhood, socialization, and so forth, but that the *self-knowledge* of one's own sociability has entirely different causes. We shall also find that the confusing of these two aspects makes it difficult for the psychologist to think clearly about the outcomes, that is, the behavioral results of self-knowledge.

Chapter 4 delves into the question of the individual's cognitive access to self-components. It is easy to say, "If you want to know something about a person's inner psychological life, just go to the person and ask directly. People know themselves better than others know them." This chapter tries to demonstrate that only the most naive psychology would undertake such a procedure in trying to get at self-knowledge. The answers that are produced by such a form of questioning, aside from how much faith the psychologist has in the style of questioning, seldom have much to do with the respondent's actual behavioral potential or cognizing of that potential. The chapter also deals with the topic of how to remedy such methods, enabling the researcher or practitioner to gain a more accurate look into existing self-components, as well as suggestions for bringing self-knowledge about. Finally, the cultural and historical roots of self-knowledge considerations are considered briefly.

Chapter 5 continues the theme of problems associated with trying to establish whether self-knowledge is "really" there, inside the person. In this chapter, the observer (i.e., the psychological researcher or the therapist) moves into the center of the analysis. The main finding of this chapter is that the observer who needs to control another person is particularly susceptible to erroneous judgments about that other's self-knowledge. Research findings, from both social-psychological and clinical areas, point to the interesting paradox that controllable or obedient others are assumed to have more self-knowledge than people who are in fact more independent. Thus, the chapter puts the observer into a paradoxical dilemma: The more interest someone has in gaining control over another, the more *actual* autonomy or *actual* self-determination will be disregarded as a criterion of self-knowledge. In their place, the criterion of "controllability for the observer" becomes the starting point for the ascription of self-knowledge.

Beginning with Chapter 6, we turn to the issue of how self-knowledge can be defined, conceptualized, researched, and applied in a systematic way. Assuming that the several varieties of the usual "self-knower school" do not offer the scientist or practitioner a sensible grasp of the self-knowledge concept, it is only sensible to turn toward more systematic treatments of the topic.

The first of these systematic positions, spelled out in the sixth chapter, is a highly conservative position. Here, we find self-knowledge defined via a person's overt behaviors. According to this view, people are not presumed to guide their behavior by self-related thoughts, and it is not presumed that a conscious sense of "who I am" precedes or accompanies sequences of behaviors. Rather, the self-knowledge issue first comes to the fore when people are asked about self-aspects—attitudes or personality traits. Then, it is assumed that, to answer such questions, they think of concrete behavioral instances that are relevant, for instance, "How often at recent parties did I demonstrate sociable behaviors?" Once this behavioral search is undertaken, they answer the question (e.g., "How sociable are you?") by making an inference from the frequency of their sociable-appearing behaviors.

Chapter 7 brings us into a more socially based view of the beginnings of self-knowledge. This chapter entertains the possibility that self-knowledge has a close relationship to the language, and that the way in which people learn to apply labels to the self defines, for individuals, their self-knowledge. For example, a white person who grows up in a predominantly black culture would quickly acquire the label *minority* and, along with it, perhaps such labels as *exotic, unusual,* and *strange*. In the more usual example, a black grows up in the midst of a very dominant white community and is thus labeled from the broader social milieu as *minority, exotic, unusual,* or *strange*. In sharp contrast to the position elucidated in Chapter 6, Chapter 7 leaves aside the observation of one's own behavior and places its focus on the labels that come to be applied as a result of social influence. In the sense of this chapter, self-knowledge is treated as coming to "know" oneself through the perspective and influence of the social milieu.

The eighth chapter continues the theme of self-knowledge within a social-influence context but takes the concepts *self* and *knowledge* more literally than do the preceding two chapters. The self is regarded as sets of behavioral potentials, and it is assumed that behavioral potentials can frequently be traced through systematic influences to their social roots. Second, self-knowledge is equated with cognizing one's own behavioral potential. The implication is that one cannot cognize, or "know," the entire self at one time, nor does it make much sense to speak of the total person as a self-knowing unity. Rather, the analysis treats each instance of a self-component, and the direct cognizing of that component, as a psychological condition of self-knowledge. The chapter then spells out the psychological ramifications of such self-cognizing in terms of self-evaluation, affect, physiology, and particularly civilized behavior.

Chapter 9 leads the reader into a curious implication of the preceding systematic positions. Common sense, earlier psychology, and particularly the usual self-knower schools have perpetuated the view of the self-knower as a mature, autonomous, creative, individualistic, not-controlled person. This picture has characteristically been forwarded as the image of the healthy person: "If we can only come into contact with our 'true, inner selves,' our problems will be solved; we will no longer be torn by conflicting social pressures, and we will have our 'own' sense of direction." But it is not so. The best possible evidence that can be assembled shows that self-knowledge, in the scientific sense of self-cognizing, produces a *controllable* being—a reliable product of everyday civilization. How does this process work?

The latter part of this book points toward the origins of that entity that is normally called the self, and the reader will find that much of this self—the behavioral potential of the individual—has a social basis. All conceivable influences, from childhood experiences to immediate social pressures, bear on the individual's behavioral potential at any given moment. Therefore, if attention is turned to the self—if this socially based self becomes increasingly cognized by the individual—the resulting knowledge is a knowledge of what society has built into the individual. And insofar as this self-knowledge results in certain behaviors, leanings, or habits, these tendencies can, in turn, be traced to the person's social origins. Thus, our conclusion is that self-knowledge in no way frees the individual from societal constraints; on the contrary, it brings the person under societal control.

CHAPTER 2

GETTING CLEAR ABOUT THE DIFFERENCE BETWEEN THE SELF AND SELF-KNOWLEDGE

From our perspective, it would appear that *self* and *knowledge of the self* are characteristically rolled into a unit, following this simple formula: If a person possesses a certain desired characteristic, such as tolerance, others then conclude that the person is aware of that tolerance. Or if a person appears to manifest patience, it is further assumed that the person *is aware* of that patience.

In fact, the reasoning generally takes a further, still more risky step: If the person manifests such ideal self-aspects as tolerance and patience, others are inclined to assume that the person is *in all respects* aware of the self, self-insightful, and the like. And on the contrary, if the person manifests the opposite qualities (intolerance and impatience), self-knowledge is no longer ascribed.

Seen from a psychologist's perspective, the above sorts of reasoning amount to a particularly blatant error. In principle, we can speak of a person's possessing tolerance or intolerance quite independent of that person's *knowledge* of being tolerant or intolerant. Let us be more graphic and spell out the logical possibilities. Someone can be tolerant, in the sense of having a readiness to allow others to go their own way, and can, at the same time, be highly aware of that tendency or else relatively unaware of that tendency. Likewise, a person can be fully intolerant and either very aware of those inclinations or seemingly unattuned to them.

This all seems plausible enough, but curiously, the psychology of self-knowledge has been completely insensitive to this sorting out and, instead, has pushed the dimensions *self* (e.g., the possession of tolerance versus intolerance) and *self-knowledge* (lesser or greater knowledge of one's own tolerance/intolerance) together into one unit. In the following, we show what this error looks like, and more important, we try to introduce the reader to some psychological notions about how to study and employ *self* and *self-knowledge* as two dimensions that are independent of one another.

LAWRENCE KOHLBERG

We may illustrate the usual fallacy with an analogy that stems from a consideration of Kohlberg's theorizing on moral development (1980). Kohlberg described approximately six stages of moral development, a progression from total dependence on specific others (Stage 1) to a seemingly advanced, autonomous morality (Stage 5 or 6). At these higher stages, the moral individual is presumed to be independent of others' influence in matters of moral judgment. The basis of each moral judgment is then said to lie inside the person; the person knows automatically how to decide and act in moral dilemmas.

Logically enough (and if we disregard Kohlberg temporarily), any given autonomous individual could have incorporated very different moral principles from those of other autonomous individuals. One person can represent the moral of extreme tolerance and antipunitiveness, and the other may embody a morality of strictness, the frequent use of punishment, and little tolerance. Is one person more autonomous than the other? Viewing the problem logically, we have to answer, "Of course not." Autonomous is autonomous. That is, a person who can exercise consistent moral judgments without reliance on others' help or influence may well represent a consistent morality of tolerance or laissez-faire but could just as easily represent a consistent morality of intolerance and punitiveness.

But Kohlberg (1980) would have it otherwise. The person who has reached the ideal Stage 5 or 6 is allowed only the option of espousing a humanitarian, highly democratic, tolerant set of values. The other logical possibility—a Stage 5 or 6 person who embodies a punitive philosophy— is explicitly ruled out. The result? Two concepts—*autonomy* and the *content of the person's morality*—are blurred together. In Kohlberg's view, the progression through the stages, upward toward Stage 6, is simultaneously a progression toward a humanitarian philosophy.

The unfortunate result is that it becomes nearly impossible for interested researchers, theorists, or practitioners to think clearly about *causality* within Kohlberg's system. Common sense would tell us that autonomy (i.e., independence of others' influence) has its roots, and the researcher may well want to study the background factors responsible for autonomy. Common sense also indicates that the content of a person's moral values (e.g., conservative or liberal) also has specifiable origins. Obviously, the researcher should be interested in studying a person's gradual progress toward a left-wing or right-wing set of values, and in tracing the causal factors.

But Kohlberg's system equates a cluster of values (humanitarian, tolerant) with autonomy and leaves us in the position of not being able to look at their separate origins. If we accept Kohlberg's reasoning, these two elements—autonomy and the content of one's morality—no longer have distinguishable antecedents. Interestingly, Kohlberg himself performed no causal analysis of the progression from Stage 1 to Stage 6. It all seems to happen "automatically."

WILLIAM JAMES AND CARL G. LANGE

An analogous case is seen in the James–Lange theory of emotion (James, 1884; Lange, 1885). James (1884) regarded the emotions as being rooted in physiological changes, the central assumption being that each distinct emotion has its roots in the perception of the visceral, skeletal, and muscular consequences following the initial perceptual apprehension of an object. For Lange (1885), subjective sensations (emotions) were secondary effects that are caused by anomalies of vascular innervation.

According to the James–Lange idea, the physiological change automatically sets the *experience* of a specific emotion in gear. The cognition or knowledge that one is angry or sexually excited is set off by physiological arousal specific to the emotions *anger* and *sexual excitement*, respectively. One cannot talk about the cognition "I am angry" independent of its concrete accompanying physiological source.

By treating emotions in this way, the theory confuses two elements. One element is arousal or physiological change, which obviously has its own, separate causes. The other element is the cognition, or experience, which has its own origins and which comes to be associated with one form of arousal or another. In the James–Lange theory, these two elements are one and the same, as whatever causes a specific form of arousal simultaneously sets off the cognition (e.g., "I am angry"). Within the James–

Lange system, it is impossible to talk about the causes of the cognition (or experience) separately from the causes of the physiological change. Is this an error?

If we contrast the James–Lange method of doing things with the later analysis of Schachter (1964), we find that the earlier system was indeed grounded in a fallacy. Schachter also began the analysis of emotions with the concept of physiological change, but he completed the analysis by viewing the nature of the emotional *experience* (i.e., the specific cognition of *anger, sexual arousal,* and so on) as being determined by separate causes. Further, he noted that an instance of physiological change, once it goes into gear, can provide the basis for any of a number of emotional experiences. Exactly which emotion is experienced once the person is aroused depends on which emotional "label" the person brings to the arousing situation. If fear-provoking matters are highly salient, the person will experience fear; if sexual matters are highly salient, the person will experience sexual arousal.

In the Schachterian experiments (see Schachter, 1964; Schachter & Singer, 1962), arousal is brought into play by adrenaline or by other stimulants or arousing experiences (see research by Zillmann, 1978). The way in which the arousal is cognized (i.e., labeled or experienced) is brought about by an entirely different set of factors, such as the nature of the social surroundings (Schachter & Singer, 1962) or the presence of salient cues to different kinds of emotional states (Zillmann, 1978). Important here is that the Schachter and Zillmann work untangled the confusion—the previous blending of two events: arousal *per se* and the way in which a person experiences or labels that arousal.

THE SELF AND SELF-KNOWLEDGE

In the developmental example from Kohlberg, we saw that two different elements, blurred by Kohlberg, can indeed be treated as distinct, so that each has its causes. The same is true of emotions. The physiological aspect and the cognitive aspect do not have to be treated as fused or inseparable, and to be sure, once they are regarded as separable, it becomes a simple matter to discuss the background underlying each of them. The same should apply to the investigation of self-knowledge. The self, as a set of behavioral potentials, can be regarded as something with its own causal origins. Processes of learning, imitation, and related factors can lead to the person's incorporating behavior potentials such as the readiness to be aggressive, passive, or sociable, or to manifest certain fears, and so on.

Such an analysis of the person's acquiring behavioral potentials can proceed completely independently of any considerations of the person's *knowledge* about those behavioral tendencies.

But what about *self-knowledge*, that is, the person's own knowledge of those behavioral potentials? How are we to understand *knowledge* of the self as a psychological event with distinct causal roots? Let's try out some possibilities.

PERSONAL MEMORY

One seemingly all-encompassing manner of coming to terms with self-knowledge is to equate the concept with a person's memory of all past personal events. Such a research enterprise is currently under way with gusto and goes by the title *autobiographical memory* (see Bradburn, Rips, & Shevell, 1987; Cantor & Kihlstrom, 1987; Kihlstrom & Cantor, 1984; Reiser, Black & Abelson, 1985). If there is a psychological cause involved here, it is the extent to which individuals have cognitive access to events out of their personal history. For instance, the researcher may be interested in factors that would prompt a person's memory for specific events that happened in kindergarten. Although it would certainly be possible to undertake a science of autobiographical memory, the concept is too broad to correspond to our purposes here. Psychology's interest in the self has largely been an interest in the self as behavioral potential, and autobiographical memory is a research enterprise that revolves around the individual's memory of past events *per se*, aside from whether those events bear on actual behavioral potential. Thus, we need to readjust our focus and think about self-knowledge with respect to the self that consists of behavioral readiness.

SELF-KNOWLEDGE AS A LABEL FOR A BEHAVIORAL TENDENCY

We cannot be far wrong in thinking that behavioral tendencies can exist without their being describable by the individual. Obviously, small children possess hosts of behavioral tendencies (i.e., habits, dispositions, and motivated tendencies) that are in no way cognitively analyzed or interpreted by those children. Adults are not necessarily any different, although we have reason to suppose that the human gradually learns to apply names, or labels, to distinguishable behavioral tendencies (Benenson & Dweck, 1986; Miller, 1984; Rholes & Ruble, 1984).

As a simple example, a young child learns by imitation to discriminate against people from Province Z, and the discrimination takes place on many levels, that is, in words, deeds, and thoughts. These behavioral potentials, all oriented against a certain target group, do not necessarily have to be labeled by the child in order to be learned. (If we carry the analysis one step further, even dogs can learn to be prejudiced against groups that don't share the skin color of their masters.) It is not that the prejudiced actions are carried out unconsciously by the child. Our point is simply that the prejudiced child has no label to attach to this cluster of actions, words, and thoughts. They simply occur.

This picture can, of course, change. If the child's social surroundings point the child's thoughts toward the label *prejudiced* within the context of the prejudiced behavioral repertoire, the child then acquires a cognitive element to associate with the actions. This kind of language acquisition and its association with specific action tendencies may be regarded as one kind of self-knowledge. And as such, this knowledge (the label for the behavior tendency) is not the same as the self: the label is not the same as the behavioral potential. Each of the two elements has its causes; each of the two elements has its own, separate character.

When the two components are not mixed together, a scientific inquiry into self-knowledge becomes feasible. The self-components (i.e, the potentials or readiness to behave) have their own historical bases and can exist quite independently of the *knowledge* of those components. Most important, those "knowledges" also have their own causes. But this is only one way to construe self-knowledge, in the sense of a knowledge of behavioral potential. There is still another route.

SELF-KNOWLEDGE AS COGNITIVE ATTUNEMENT TO THE SELF

Once again, we can begin with the origin of behavioral tendencies: What is their background? How are they learned? Which ones are biologically determined? And then, independently of how they have come into being, we can add the knowledge element to the picture. In this case, the knowledge element is simpler than a learned semantic label; it is the turning of conscious attention to a given behavioral potential. A person's conscious attention can, of course, be directed to different events or objects and can be turned to self-aspects as well (Duval & Wicklund, 1972; Shibutani, 1961; Wolff, 1932). It is possible to name causal factors that steer a person's attention toward certain self-aspects, and these causal events are, of course, *not* the same ones that produce the manifold behavioral tendencies in the first place. Once again, we can separate (1) self-knowledge and its antecedents from the (2) self (as behavioral potential) and its antecedents.

SELF-KNOWLEDGE THEORY AS IT EXISTS IN PSYCHOLOGY: THE BLENDING AND FUSING OF TWO ELEMENTS

By now the reader should have noted the ease with which psychology can, in principle, separate self issues from self-knowledge issues. And thus occur the surprise and disappointment when we find that psychology has been singularly unsuccessful in abiding by the separation. Instead, blending and confusion have dominated. But what do blending and confusion entail? In what ways can a confusion between the self and self-knowledge come to the fore?

CONFUSING STRENGTH OF IMPULSE WITH SELF-KNOWLEDGE

Suppose that we have a group of persons who vary in terms of the strength of a behavioral tendency, such as a moral standard. Some of the people are occasionally altruistic, others are more likely to be altruistic, and a third set of individuals show altruistic reactions whenever possible. Does one group have more self-knowledge than the other? If we are convinced that the self (in this case, the extent of altruism-readiness) and self-knowledge have separate roots, in differentiable causal factors, then we would conclude that the strength of the behavioral inclination is not very informative about a person's self-knowledge.

However, we could also use the strength of the tendency as a jumping-off point to initiate some confusion. Why not simply assume that the stronger the altruism, the more the person possesses self-knowledge in the area of altruism? Or we could even state the case more strongly: The stronger the altruism, the more the person has self-knowledge *in general,* thus a sweeping, overriding kind of self-knowledge.

As it turns out, this manner of confusing the self with knowledge of the self is more often than not what we find in the self-knowledge literature. The *strength* and *content* of the self are employed as the starting point of the confusion. A person who has Inclination X is regarded as a self-knower; the person with Inclination non-X does not attain such status in the eyes of the self-knowledge theorist. This remarkable failure—a simple confusion—runs rampant through the literature and is largely responsible for the nonscientific character of self-knowledge theory in psychology. But what is the confusion all about concretely? This question brings us to the next chapter.

CHAPTER 3

THE SELF-KNOWER SCHOOL

Why "self-knower"? This term refers to a *type* of person, to individuals who have allegedly gained insight or a cognitive view into the self. These are presumably the persons whose self is no longer a mystery and who can communicate with clarity about the inner workings and components of their own being. What brings about this insight or knowledge? Is a self-knower for once and for all a self-knower? Does self-knower status have systematic ramifications for subsequent behaving and thinking? As we shall illustrate in this chapter, the dominant treatments of self-knowledge are reducible to the task of *spotting the self-knower*. Various criteria ostensibly enable the researcher to separate self-knowers from non-self-knowers, criteria that should also allow the clinician to recognize the patient who has made good progress in the direction of self-insight.

In the course of becoming absorbed with the correct criteria for spotting the self-knower, the schools of thought summarized here neglect the issues of the causal background of self-knowledge and the behavioral or thought-process consequences of self-knowledge. The ideal separation of the *self* from *knowledge of the self* is cast aside, and the end product of the approach of the self-knower school is a simple, static portrait of the hero: an idealized portrait of the self-knower. Let us look more closely at this dominant way of thinking about self-knowledge.

THE SELF-KNOWER ACCORDING TO GORDON ALLPORT

Allport (1937) accompanied his discussion of self-knowledge with a certain skepticism. He was not in agreement with the proposition that humans have direct, automatic access to a "true" self. His critique was leveled primarily at the notion of introspection; Allport simply doubted that the human functions so that a cognitive light can willfully be shone on the inner core of the person's own self.

But then, perhaps surprising the reader, he allowed that there is indeed such an entity as the self-knowing person, and that there must be criteria by which this self-knower or "self-insightful" person can be spotted or recognized. His solution is unique within the self-knower school: Persons were said by Allport to have self-knowledge (self-insight) when their reported self-view agrees with others' perceptions of them:

> How is the psychologist to tell whether an individual has insight? According to an old adage, every man has three characters:
> 1. that which he has
> 2. that which he thinks he has; and
> 3. that which others think he has.
> . . . the most predictable index becomes the ratio between the second and the third items—the relation of what a man thinks he is to what others (especially the psychologist who studies him) think he is. (Allport, 1937, p. 291)

This kind of thinking is reflected in the modern peer-rating technique (Jackson, 1967), where the opinions of a respondent's friends or other acquaintances are used as a validity criterion—as the measure of whether the respondent's self-directed statements are accurate. As a simple example, in 1974 Snyder gave a sample of subjects a "self-monitoring" questionnaire, asking them questions pertaining to their tendencies to try to make good impressions, their tendencies to adjust their behaviors strategically according to the social setting, and related items. In order to get at the validity of these self-reports, the subjects' fraternity brothers were asked for their own impressions of the respondent, and in turn, the correspondence between impressions of oneself ("Do I try to impress others?") and others' impressions of oneself ("Does he try to impress others?") could be calculated. To be sure, Snyder reported considerable correspondence between these two sources of impressions about the respondent. In Allport's language, the subjects seemed to know themselves.

The Allport criterion for recognizing the self-knower places the weight of the evidence on the individual's social surroundings. Divorcing himself totally from the idea of direct, introspective access into the self, Allport allowed self-knowers to be defined on a social level—on the plane of agreement between persons and their observers.

Is this the best approach? An obvious point of criticism is that outside observers have no better access to the individual's "inner core" than do the individuals themselves. Such agreement between self-observer and external observer may come about simply via social influence: if the person is skillful in portraying certain personal qualities, then the surrounding community will find those portrayals plausible—hence the agreement between person and society that forces the conclusion that the person is a self-knower (Swann, 1983).

Allport was the only member of the self-knower school who used a pure social criterion of self-knowingness. The other representatives of this school of thought have openly rejected such a position and have paid heed only to individual qualities, always pushing the role of society to the background. Interestingly, Allport (1937) also allowed that self-knowledge might be recognizable by such individual characteristics, observing that psychologists know that certain personal facets correlate with self-knowledge. The self-knower (Allport's mature person) is said to

> (1) have a widely extended sense of self; (2) be able to relate himself warmly to others in both intimate and nonintimate contacts; (3) possess a fundamental emotional security and accept himself; (4) perceive, think, and act with zest in accordance with outer reality; (5) be capable of self-objectivation, of insight and humor; (6) live in harmony with a unifying philosophy of life. (Allport, 1937, p. 307)

How did Allport know that the person with high security or with a good sense of humor also possesses self-knowledge? It is all true by definition. There is simply a gradation of individuals, ranging from not-self-knowing to highly self-knowing or insightful; those toward the higher end of the continuum have humor and security. This position comes close to the standpoint of three clinically oriented schools that are very much in the center of the self-knower school. What do they look like in detail?

THE SELF-KNOWER ACCORDING TO SIDNEY JOURARD

"Avoids the use of social facades" is one of the signs of self-knowingness listed by Allport (1942). There is a certain common sense behind this criterion, which, in the words of Jourard and Lasakow (1958), is characterized as the absence of a "marketing personality," that is, freedom from "self-alienation." The basic idea is a simple one: To the degree that a person's actions appear to be shaped by the immediate society and are thus responsive to the marketplace, to modes, to conformity pressures, that person's actions obviously do not reflect the *true* self.

Jourard (1958) regards self-insight as a prerequisite to mental health and assumes that the self-insightful person can be recognized by the criterion of readiness to self-disclose to others in an *accurate* manner. And at the same time, self-disclosure is also the instrument—the means to the desired end of self-knowledge and normality:

... accurate portrayal of the self to others is an identifying criterion of healthy
personality, while neurosis is related to inability to know one's "real self" and
to make it known to others. (Jourard & Lasakow, 1958, p. 91)

Thus, the ideal individual to whom Jourard refers becomes evident. The
normal personality is at the same time a self-knowing personality. Self-
knowing is not agreement with others, but the leaving aside of social
facades and the open reporting to others of one's true inner self.

The reader should not jump to the conclusion that the Jourard-styled
self-knower is a self-centered blabbermouth. On the contrary, the self-
disclosure must have a certain socially acceptable quality. One constraint
on the style of the self-discloser is formulated by Waterman (1979), who
interpreted Jourard as referring to a "congruent" mode of communication.
Optimal self-disclosure is said to entail a clear message about the speaker's
feelings and thoughts in which verbal content and nonverbal cues match
(Waterman, 1979, pp. 234–235). Similarly, Chelune (1979) observed that
too much (or too little) disclosure in a given setting was thought by Jourard
to be indicative of disturbance in the self and in interpersonal relationships. The relationship between self-disclosure and mental health is appar-
ently curvilinear. The message here is clear enough: The self-knower talks
about the self, but within the constraints of civilized society. On the other
hand, doesn't the acknowledgment of such constraints imply that the
Jourard self-knower is perhaps offering little more than a socially desirable
facade?

QUANTIFYING THE SELF-KNOWER

Not content with a mere set of assumptions about the characteristics
of the normal, self-knowing individual, Jourard and Lasakow (1958) developed a procedure for tapping into their respondents' readiness to self-
disclose. The first step was to draw up a list of self-facets that might
conceivably be disclosed (communicated about) to others. Proceeding
quite systematically, Jourard and Lasakow defined six areas that they
deemed self-pertinent:

1. Attitudes and opinions.
2. Tastes and interests.
3. Work or studies.
4. Money.
5. Personality.
6. Body.

Within each area 10 subtopics were listed, for example, "my views on
communism," "my personal opinions and feelings about other religious

groups than my own, e.g., Protestants, Catholics, Jews, atheists," or "my feelings about different parts of my body—legs, hips, waist, chest, or bust, etc." (p. 92). For each of 60 topics, the subjects were requested to state how much they had communicated about it to others—to their mothers, their fathers, a male friend, a female friend, and their spouses. A three-step scale was used to allow subjects to reflect their degree of self-disclosure:

0 = "Have told the other person nothing about this aspect of me."
1 = "Have talked in general terms about this item. The other person has only a general idea about this aspect of me."
2 = "Have talked in full and complete detail about this item to the other person. He knows me fully in this respect, and could describe me accurately." (Jourard & Lasakow, 1958, p. 91)

Jourard and Lasakow then proceeded to derive a total self-disclosure score for each of their more than 300 subjects. Although there was no reason to suspect any special differences within the sample, they found that white subjects had higher self-disclosure scores than blacks, and that women reported more self-disclosing than men. In a subsequent study using the same kind of procedure, Jourard (1961) observed that respondents from the United States were more self-disclosing than the respondents in an English sample.

What Psychological Facets Are Reflected in the Measurement?

Jourard (1961) took the measure seriously as an empirical reflection of the person's attained level of self-disclosure, thus as a reflection of the person's normality and self-knowingness. According to his theoretical assumption, the suppression or repression of self-related thoughts is reflected in the withholding of disclosures from others. It then follows that certain cultures "which produce modal personalities with differing self-disclosure habits might well produce different frequencies for certain kinds of illness" (p. 320). The message is clear: Jourard had sufficient faith in his theoretical premise and in the measuring device so that he was prepared to hint that certain kinds of mental illness should be more prevalent in England than in the United States.

But there is a quirk in the story: In 1969, Hurley and Hurley undertook a further study, using Jourard's technique, but they also obtained observer ratings of each subject's tendency to self-disclose. (This latter was called the Direct Disclosure Rating, or DDR.) These DDR ratings were obtained within ongoing groups, so that the members rated each others' disclosure tendencies following group interaction. It turned out that the relation between the person's own claimed disclosure rate (the Jourard measure) and the DDR was almost nonexistent; that is, the correlation between the two was −.10. Does this mean that the group really did not understand the individual's true disclosure tendencies? If we take Allport's first self-knowledge criterion seriously (agreement between self-ratings and others' ratings), we must conclude that the participants in the Hurley and Hurley study possessed approximately *zero* self-knowledge. However, in the Jourard school and in several more to be discussed in this chapter, considerably less weight is attached to the role of others' opinions in relation to one's own self-knowledge.

This rejection of social influence, in the sense that social pressures can only interfere with one's finding one's "true" self, is a dominant theme in a number of therapeutic schools, as documented by Wallach and Wallach (1983). Since the early 1950s, according to Wallach and Wallach, certain segments of clinical and developmental psychology have emphasized the psychological health implications of being *authentic*, true to one's inner being, actualized with respect to one's individual potential, and the like. Accompanying this theoretical orientation is a rejection of others, of communications, or of social influence as potential sources of one's makeup. Self-oriented thoughts and communications are, within these schools of thought, the only route to finding one's authentic self. This philosophy becomes still more pronounced as we move on to the next two contributions.

THE SELF-KNOWER ACCORDING TO CARL ROGERS

The pushing aside of socially steered, facadelike behavior was central for Rogers (1950, 1951), whose contribution antedated that of Jourard. Rogers drew a sharp line of demarcation between the person as an embodiment of societal standards and the person as a reflection of the "true self." This distinction is reflected vividly in Rogers's views of social influence in general (it can be said to often result in facadelike behavior) and of education. For Rogers (1951), the purpose of democratic education is to "assist" students to "become individuals who are able to take self-initiated action and to be responsible for these actions" (p. 387) and "who are capable of intelligent choice and self-direction" (p. 387). Nowhere in Rogers's writings is there any acknowledgment of society's role in building values, morals, or philosophies into the individual. All of these develop, somehow naturally, out of a God-given, organic core of the self.

A core assumption in Rogers's thinking is that the inner kernel of the person is "positive," this positivity stemming directly from each person's nature. The kernel itself is depicted as a dynamic, organismic, experiencing process. If a person is fortunate enough to gain experiential access to this kernel, the person may then be classified as "real" and as "congruent," as opposed to presenting a socially based facade (Zurhorst, 1983).

What kinds of preconditions are then conducive to the individual's coming to be a ripe, responsible person, with insight into the self? Rogers's analysis allows that those who are surrounded by a permissive atmosphere, who are accorded responsibility for their own actions, and who are granted "basic respect" will develop a sense of responsible self-direction as well as enhanced creativity and a number of other by-products, all of these effects accompanying magnified insight into the self.

The writings of Rogers are replete with indices by which one can spot the self-knower; a somewhat representative list reads:

- Ability to consider one's own abilities with more objectivity.
- Perception of oneself as more independent.
- Perception of oneself as more spontaneous.
- Perception of oneself as more genuine.
- Perception of oneself as more integrated and less divided.

Although these criteria are somewhat different from those of Allport and Jourard, the theoretical point is the same. One can recognize the self-knower by means of the person's manifestation of certain valued traits—at least traits that are valued in an academically or therapeutically oriented subgroup, within a modern, technically oriented society.

Faith in the respondent's self-reports is a further earmark of Rogers's approach: "The client is the only one who has the potentiality of knowing fully the dynamics of his perceptions and his behavior" (1951, p. 221). We have already seen that this kind of assumption got Jourard into trouble in his attempt to assess self-knowledge (self-disclosing) via self-reports of one's past. Nonetheless, this axiom is important to almost all self-knower schools, and the theme will become more pronounced as we move toward Chapter 4.

QUANTIFYING THE SELF-KNOWER

One early effort to objectify the effects of Rogerian therapy, and thus to identify the self-knowing, healthy individual, is attributable to Walker, Rablen, and Rogers (1960). The idea is that the patient at early stages (i.e., the non-self-knowing person) is somewhat rigid, closed, and lacking in spontaneity. Such shortcomings can be characterized along seven dimensions ("strands" in the words of Walker *et al.*), these being:

1. Feelings and personal meanings.
2. Experiencing.

3. Incongruence.
4. Communication of self.
5. Construing the experience.
6. Relation to problems.
7. Manner of relating.

The patient at earlier stages—or more generally, the non-self-knower—is regarded as unexpressive with respect to feelings, is unaware of the experiencing process, does not communicate about the self effectively (cf. Jourard), does not recognize problems, and avoids intimacy (cf. Jourard).

The study involved the examination of six transcribed cases from a university counseling center. Following each of the patients through the course of treatment by means of the protocols, the raters evaluated the patients' progress, using the seven factors ("strands"). The reported reliability between the two raters was quite high. More concretely, this means that the two raters agreed on the progress of Patient X with respect to self-oriented communications or with regard to the patient's manner of relating.

The procedure allowed the authors to draw conclusions about the validity of this kind of method. It turned out that the raters' progress ratings for the individual patients corresponded reasonably well to the third author's (Rogers's) independent assessment of the patients' progress in therapy.

The technique explored by Walker *et al.* looks at the individual's growth in the direction of self-knowledge in terms of seven dimensions. A subsequent study by Kiesler, Mathieu, and Klein (1964) took a similar tack: The protocols of former therapy sessions were examined by raters. This time, however, the raters' focus was on just one of the dimensions—experiencing—which is said to be pivotal in Rogers's scheme of things. Following the Rogerian line of thought, Kiesler *et al.* referred to "experiencing" as

> The degree to which the client manifests Inward Reference in his verbalizations. The client is referring inwardly when he is referring to his own feelings and reactions—when he is searching for the meaning of the personal events, feelings, and ideas he is reporting. (p. 350)

At the bottom end of the rating scale used in the study is the level of "no personal involvement." This is defined as the absence of personal references and refusal of personal involvement. At the top end of the dimension is the "high-experiencing" individual: feelings come to the fore of the communication; the client can "travel freely among feelings and understands them quickly"; and "He moves easily from one inward reference to another and is able to integrate them into his experiential frame of reference" (p. 350). Experiencing is, then, the attainment of a flowing, highly verbalizable knowledge of one's own feelings.

Just as in the Walker *et al.* procedure, the raters in the Kiesler *et al.* study evidenced a strong reliability; that is, they seemed to agree on the definition of "experiencing" and could extract approximately the same sense from the protocols.

What Psychological Facets Are Reflected in the Measurement?

If the theory is correct, then the therapy sessions should lead to an enhanced self-knowledge, that is, to heightened experiencing scores as judged by the raters. Remarkably enough, the results of Kiesler *et al.* showed the *opposite:* as therapy proceeded, the experiencing scores dropped. A further extrapolation of the theory: At the very beginning stages of therapy neurotic subjects should evidence *less* experiencing than normal subjects (the study also included normal subjects who had participated in quasitherapy sessions). But the data show otherwise: at the outset of the sessions, there was scarcely any difference between the experiencing levels of schizophrenic and normal subjects, whereas neurotic respondents showed considerably *more* experiencing than did the normals and the schizophrenics. The same pattern of differences holds up during the course of the sessions.

In other words, the tendency to reflect self-orientation with respect to feelings was highest at the outset of therapy, not at the end. Further, the tendency to reflect self-orientation with regard to feelings was highest among the sample categorized as neurotic. All of this leads one to think that "normality" and "experiencing" may not be one and the same, and that, in fact, there may well be some active opposition between the two. The empirical facts are not as simple as Rogers's characterization of things.

THE SELF-KNOWER ACCORDING TO ABRAHAM MASLOW

"Self-actualization" is the central personal goal in Maslow's theoretical scheme. A certain natural development of strength, and of one's potential, is a theme common in Maslow's writings (1961). The attaining of certain "peak experiences" is said to be the ideal:

> The person in the peak-experience usually feels himself to be at the peak of his powers, using all of his capacities at the best and fullest. In Rogers' nice phrase, he feels "fully-functioning." He feels more intelligent, more perspective, wittier, stronger, or more graceful than at other times. He is at his best, at concert pitch, at the top of his form. This is not only felt subjectively but can be seen by the observer. (Maslow, 1968, p. 276)

The overlap with both Jourard and Rogers, and in part with Allport ("intelligent, witty"), is evident, in that people who are in contact with their true selves are judged to be so on the basis of their positive standing on numerous socially valued dimensions. Once again, the self-knower is spotted on the basis of a number of easy-to-recognize socially desirable characteristics. But Maslow carried the story still further: The actualized individual (the self-knower) turns into a highly motivated, unstoppable, self-righteous dynamic. In Maslow's language (1968), "There are then no glancing blows . . . only full hits" (p. 276). Maslow proceeded with the list:

> feels himself to be his own boss, fully responsible, fully volitional . . . more decisive, looking more strong, more single-minded, more apt to scorn or overcome opposition, more grimly sure of himself, more apt to give the impression that it would be useless to try to stop him . . . free of blocks, inhibitions, . . . self-criticism . . . more spontaneous . . . unguarded . . . more natural (simple, relaxed, unhesitant, plain, sincere, unaffected, primitive in a particular sense). (pp. 276–277)

As exemplars of self-actualized individuals, Maslow (1977) brought certain sets of heroes to the forefront, people who ostensibly embody the several characteristics by which the Maslowian self-knower is spotted. The champions in his wax museum of self-actualizers include Abraham Lincoln, Thomas Jefferson, Eleanor Roosevelt, Albert Einstein, Albert Schweitzer, and William James. We are led to think that these are the classic models of individuals who came to know and to develop—to the fullest—their true selves. These are people who were spontaneous, simple, relaxed, plain, intelligent, creative, sure of themselves, not suppressed, and the like. One notes in Maslow's list that self-actualization appears to be almost exclusively a North American characteristic or, at least, a trait of people who immigrated to North America. Of course, the view is similar to Jourard's (1961): The American culture is said to have more potential for true self-expression than that of England or Germany.

Just as with Jourard and Rogers, the self-knower here is seemingly free of the dictates and influences of everyday society. Much of the authentic contact with the self is seen as being accompanied by the discarding of socially rooted facades or false values. Maslow's term for abiding by these "false," externally imposed values is "authoritarian." This autonomous essence of the self-knower is reflected also in Kohlberg's model of morality stages (1980), in which the lower (immature) stages entail the person's sheepishly abiding by the wishes of concrete others, and the highest moral levels are characterized by the person's autonomous development of principles that are not simply derivatives of the usual social rules. Self-actualized persons are thus autonomous, spontaneous individuals who have come to know their true and innate potentials.

QUANTIFYING THE SELF-KNOWER

A Maslowian scholar, Shostrom (1963), is regarded as the main operationalizer of Maslow's thinking. It was Shostrom who tried to bring Maslow's ideas within the paper-and-pencil reach of the common person. We will discuss briefly an empirical project by Knapp, Shostrom, and Knapp (1978), which offers an overview of the manner in which self-actualizing is made concrete.

In a characteristic example, in assessing a person's autonomy the following two alternatives are offered to the respondent:

1. I live by values which are in agreement with others.
2. I live by values which are primarily based on my own feelings.

In addition to *autonomy*, the complete measure also includes *existentiality* (ability to react without rigid adherence to principles), *feeling reactivity* (sensitivity to one's own moods and feelings), *spontaneity*, and *self-worth*. (The reader may note a strong overlap with the characteristics of the Rogerian self-knower.) The interpersonal side is also assessed (as by Jourard and Rogers), under the title of *capacity for intimate contact*.

In an attempt to prove the validity of this system, "several prominent psychologists" (Knapp et al., 1978, p. 107) were asked to nominate a group of actualized persons who were to be the respondents in the study, as well as a group of nonactualized persons, also to be respondents. Obviously, Einstein and Eleanor Roosevelt were not among those nominated, but presumably the prominent psychologists found others, a bit less actualized, in their midst. In turn, each of the persons filled out the scale, and to be sure, the people who were nominated as actualized evidenced the most positive scale scores: they claimed more autonomy, they allowed themselves more intimate contact, and so forth. In another study (Fox, Knapp, & Michael, 1968), hospitalized psychiatric patients were shown to produce lower self-actualizing scores.

What Psychological Facets Are Reflected in the Measurement?

Just as with the measurement techniques in the Jourard and Rogers approaches, the set of items here is assumed (at least for some of the items) to tap directly into subjects' self-knowledge. The ripe, experienced, actualized subjects are recognized via their reports of being able to experience emotions, self-confidence, spontaneity, and the like. Maslow (1971; see Knapp et al., 1978, p. 134) willingly accepted the scale as a fair empirical definition of his manifold characterization of the self-actualizer: "Self-actualization can now be defined quite operationally, as intelligence tests used to be defined, that is, self-actualization is what that test tests" (Maslow, 1971, p. 28). On the other hand, the test places complete faith in the self-report accuracies of individuals, in their skills in being able to follow their own psychological processes. We saw that this was a problem in Jourard's own scale, and later in this book (Chapter 4), we shall find that this is a stumbling block within the self-knower school in general.

CERTAIN ESOTERIC THERAPIES: A CONTINUATION OF THE SELF-KNOWER THEME

Assagioli (1973) introduced a method into the literature referred to as *psychosynthesis*, an approach that reflects much of the thinking of the self-knower schools. The starting point is the person's experiencing a so-called existential crisis, in which present values do not seem to lead to happiness or success. The answer to such crises, just as with Maslow or Rogers, is a deeper probing and exploring of the true self.

As in the other approaches, Assagioli regarded the person-in-crisis as beset by too many dominant social roles or facades. These societal expectations, or roles, are referred to by Assagioli as "subpersonalities." When we become too strongly identified with such subpersonalities (e.g., "I am a salesperson"), we can no longer separate our true selves from that role, social demand, or "subpersonality." The goal is to gain a more direct contact with the true center of the self. In the words of Crampton (1981):

> as the center of identity shifts from the "I" toward the Self, the person is increasingly in touch with the creative will of the Self and experiences the personality as his or her vehicle of expression. (p. 723)

What facilitates the person's moving toward this autonomous, conscious relationship with the self? One of the techniques associated with Assagioli is called the *evocation of inner wisdom*. The patient is asked to take up an inner dialogue with a figure that is ostensibly a source of wisdom. This figure is to be selected freely by the patient and may be an elder, spiritual teacher, a sacred animal, an element in nature, or an abstract symbol. (The idea is not without foundation: in the Grimm fairy tales, children confronted with awesome terror often take refuge in the world of animals.) The mission of this wisdom figure is to allow patients an outside perspective on their existence. Through the perspective of this wise figure, patients are increasingly able to uncover the subpersonalities and the false identifications, and to come more quickly to a sense of their true inner being.

Once again, we see two dominant elements in the context of self-knowledge. The true self is regarded as a unity, as a core element within the individual that is not to be broken into separate elements. Second, the true self is to be differentiated unequivocally from the "subpersonalities," that, is from the false identifications with roles, the superficial or facadelike social identities.

Also within the context of the self-knower school, Forisha (1981) wrote a summary statement on the requisite elements of a feminist psychotherapy. It is charged that many problems of women derive from over-socialization into the receptive role of a woman, and that these social influences have robbed women of their essential selves. Required is a *resocialization* into a more modern world and, of course, a detachment from previously incorporated cultural norms:

> Such resocialization requires an understanding of the realistic options offered by society; an awareness of the learned patterns and internalized norms acquired in previous socialization; a knowledge of self, one's talents, abilities, limitations, and potential for growth. (Forisha, 1981, p. 319)

Just as with Rogers, Maslow, Jourard, and Assagioli, this freeing of oneself from the facades of societally defined roles and movement toward one's "real" self requires some assistance from the outside. In the present case, the route to self-knowledge is said to proceed through acknowledging one's own anger (cf. Maslow, 1961), learning to take care of oneself, and sensing one's own autonomy. A therapist is given the responsibility of steering the patient in these directions, obviously without forcing any new doctrines on the patient. No matter which self-knowledge school we deal with, the discovering of the true self is something that clients accomplish under their own steam.

How is the self-knower recognized? Although no scales or other empirical instruments are offered by Forisha, it is evident enough that the criterion of such self-knowledge is the manifestation of a new set of attitudes toward the self and toward society. Self-knowing is reflected in an enhanced sense of power, a sense of being liberated, a refusal to accept roles that carry the label *traditional*.

A CONTINUOUS THEME OF SELFISHNESS?

Self-actualization, self-discovering, finding the authentic self, and similar concepts can certainly be viewed as a form of egocentric or selfish behavior (Wallach & Wallach, 1983). Wallach and Wallach characterized self-actualized or authentic people, particularly from the perspectives of Maslow and Rogers, as

> "not dependent for their main satisfactions on the real world, or other people or culture." . . . the environment should be "primarily a means to the person's self-actualizing ends."
>
> The same concern for autonomy enabled Rogers to come to feel that the only real criterion for an individual to consider is whether something makes him or her "a richer, more complete, more fully developed person." (p. 165)

On the other hand, the self-knower school—particularly the versions of Jourard, Maslow, Rogers, and the new therapy forms just reviewed—also insists that the actualized person, the self-knower, has an improved sense of relations with others. Wallach and Wallach found these two views— living for oneself and the betterment of interpersonal relations—to be mutually contradictory:

> As we see it, Maslow and Rogers and many other psychologists at the present time are so concerned about potential threats to freedom and autonomy that they attempt to shield us from external influence to a degree far beyond what is in fact good for us. Although it is true that misuses of authority are legion, it does not follow that all authority is illegitimate and to be avoided—such as that of all team coaches and orchestra conductors, or that of all parents, teachers, and judges. (p. 168)

Wallach and Wallach have spotted a contradiction, or at least a paradox, within the humanistic self-knower school. The only defense of the self-knower school lies in the insistence that a self-oriented person, whose thoughts and verbiage are highly self-directed, will be more interested in the welfare of other human beings. In short, the individual is being asked, within the self-knower schools just summarized, to discover a self that does *not* have its roots in societal values. In turn, once this true, *a*social self is known, the person is supposed to be better equipped to deal with other people.

THE SELF-KNOWER ACCORDING TO PAUL WARSHAW AND FRED DAVIS

A relatively simple conception of self-knowledge was offered in 1984 by Warshaw and Davis. The self-knower is again in the center of the picture, but this time there is little philosophical buildup. Rather, the contribution revolves around an empirical study, and only two characteristics of the self-knower are brought into focus: (1) consistency between word and deed and (2) the description of oneself as a self-knower.

The starting point was the classification of research subjects along a dimension of self-knowingness; this was accomplished in a refreshingly naive, straightforward manner, in that the subjects were asked to state, along an 11-step scale, how well they "understand themselves." The next step was to determine whether the high self-knowers were also generally more consistent in behaving. For instance, when someone claims to attend sports events frequently, does that person then *in fact* do so with great frequency?

For this latter information, Warshaw and Davis relied on two kinds of self-reports from their subjects. First of all, the subjects had to indicate the likelihood that they would attend sports events or go to the pub (or participate in a variety of other activities) within the next several days. Then, after a sufficient interval, the subjects returned and were asked how often they had gone to the pub and so forth. Based on these two kinds of self-reports, Warshaw and Davis computed a consistency index for each subject. For instance, if a subject said that he planned to go to the tavern once a week and then later reported that he had been to the tavern once a week, his consistency was, by definition, high. On the theoretical side, then, the Warshaw and Davis argument is that self-knowing people are consistent in their actions and words; on the empirical side, one can spot the self-knower through self-descriptions ("I understand myself") and through self-reported consistency.

Unfortunately, as has so often been the case in the empirical examples we have examined, Warshaw and Davis's expectations just did not work out. The greatest consistency was reported by subjects whose self-knowledge fell in the middle range. After this group came the "high self-knowers," and finally, the low self-knowers manifested the least consistency. The reader might well want to criticize this study on the grounds that consistency was based in self-reports of behaving, and that there was no information available about whether the subjects were, in fact, more, or less, consistent. But leaving this kind of critique aside for a moment (cf. Chapter 4), one at least sees the kind of portrait of the human that Warshaw and Davis offered. A given individual is either a self-knower or not, certain characteristics tell us about the person's self-knower status, and the individual is treated as a self-knowing unit. There is no differentiation among different facets of the self. This brings us to the next self-knower school, where one sees, for the first time in this chapter, a differentiation among parts of the self.

THE SELF-KNOWER ACCORDING TO HAZEL MARKUS

Central to Markus's treatment of the self-knowledge concept (1983) is the idea that self-knowledge can be divided into different knowledge realms. For instance, one can have self-knowledge of "preferences and values, of goals and motives, and of rules and strategies for regulating and controlling behavior" (p. 544). Markus found it inadequate to ask the individual, in blanket form, such questions as "Who are you?" Rather, one must address such specific components as rules or strategies for behavior in different realms.

The connection between self-knowledge and the person's behaving is also spelled out, in the form of a general hypothesis. It is proposed that the more self-relevant a domain is, and thus the more self-knowledge a person should have in that domain, the more individuals will understand the causes and consequences of their actions in those same domains. An artist with a great deal of experience would be regarded as having more artist-relevant self-knowledge than someone who is artistically disinclined. And artists, at least in the behavioral realms directly pertinent, are assumed to have greater insight into the antecedents of their own artistic behaviors and the psychological processes that accompany them. However, the artist does not necessarily have self-knowledge in such unpracticed areas as foreign languages; in stumbling through a language in a foreign tongue, the artist should, according to Markus, have little insight into what transpires during the attempt to speak.

We can paint the picture still more fully: If a person has self-knowledge in a given domain, then the person will (1) process information about the self more efficiently in that domain; (2) be more consistent in responding; (3) have better recall of information in that domain; (4) predict self-initiated actions in that domain; (5) resist new information that runs counter to one's self-concept in that domain; and (6) better evaluate the relevance of new information to that domain (Markus, 1983, p. 548; also in Markus & Sentis, 1982).

Where does self-knowledge come from? Markus hinted at the role of past experience in a behavioral domain, and also at the development of a sense of responsibility in a domain of behavior. However, the developmental antecedents of self-knowledge do not receive systematic treatment here, and we will not devote further speculation to the developmental issue.

Thus far, the overall picture is clear. As in the other self-knower schools, Markus's self-knowing person is regarded as manifesting certain characteristics and styles, such as being more consistent (cf. Warshaw & Davis, 1984) and processing self-relevant information within the appropriate domain more efficiently. But now comes the more concrete question: How are self-knowing individuals recognized in empirical research?

The groundwork was laid in an article by Markus in 1977, in which the term *self-schema* was used rather than *self-knowledge*. The first step is for the researcher to decide on a self-domain (e.g., athletics) that might be important to at least some respondents. Then, each potential subject is asked for two kinds of information about athletics: (1) a self-description along the dimension "athletic," (i.e., from "very athletic" to "not athletic") and (2) an indication of how important the athletic dimension is personally. Markus's assumption was that the extremity in the self-description, weighted by the importance of the dimension, provides a valid index of self-knowledge. A person who claims, for instance, to be extremely athletic and who at the same time finds sports to be important personally would be regarded as possessing self-knowledge in athletics.

One can just as well apply Markus's definitions to personality traits (e.g., open vs. not open). Let us suppose that respondents are to indicate on an 11-point scale how open they are. Someone who checks either +5 (very open) or −5 (definitely not open) and who also thinks the dimension is important would be regarded as possessing self-knowledge about the dimension *openness*. On the other hand, a respondent who checks perhaps +1, zero, or −1 would not be included among the self-knowers on this dimension.

The reader might note a small logical problem here. What becomes of persons who are sure that they are very slightly above the mid-point in openness (i.e., +1)? By Markus's extremity criterion, they cannot be regarded as having self-knowledge of that slightly-above-average level of openness. The same problem crops up when we think of self-knowledge along a political spectrum of right-wing to left-wing; a person who is middle of the road, by the extremity criterion, cannot be regarded as a self-knower.

MARKUS'S SELF-KNOWER CRITERIA COMPARED TO THE OTHER SELF-KNOWER THEORIES

Two aspects of Markus's self-knower criteria are unique among the theorists whom we examine here. (1) One aspect is an emphasis on certain information-processing capabilities. The self-knower is said to be more capable of deciding whether certain potentially self-relevant information is indeed self-relevant (a central point in empirical work by Markus, 1977), and the self-knower is also said to be more apt to resist information that does not fit the self-conception, a point documented by Sweeney and Moreland (1980). The latter point is interesting in that the self-knower of Maslow and Rogers is regarded as tending to be more open to potentially self-threatening information. Thus, the Markus version and the Maslow and Rogers versions disagree on this point of openness to self-concept-discrepant information.

(2) But there is an even more fundamental difference between Markus's criteria for self-knowledge and the criteria of Allport, Rogers, and Maslow. For the other theorists, the presence of certain positive features is the earmark of self-knowledge (e.g., a sense of humor, intelligent and creative functioning, autonomy, warmth, and self-confidence). For all of these theorists, the *direction* of the self-knower's traits is the positive or socially valued direction. Markus treated the issue in a more theoretically general manner, in proposing that persons can also have knowledge of their own ineptness, uncreativity, or stupidity. It is the *extremity* of the trait and its subjective importance that lead the Markus theorist to infer self-knowledge, not the *direction* or the social desirability of the trait.

Are Both Extremes of a Dimension Equally Self-Knowing?

In theory, the Markus system treats the two ends of a personality dimension as equivalent with respect to their potential for signaling the presence of self-knowledge. Both the extremely tolerant person and the extremely intolerant person can, theoretically, be individuals with a strong self-schema, and thus with high self-knowledge in the area of tolerance-intolerance. However, one should not forget that extremity is only one of the determining factors. The *importance* that the individual accords the trait is the second contributing factor, and it is here that we see the problems in applying the model:

Let us begin with a simple case. A person who claims to be very tolerant and who finds tolerance important would be regarded as in possession of a self-schema (i.e., as self-knowing in the tolerance area). But what happens at the other end of the continuum? Is the *in*tolerant person likely to claim that intolerance is important? Or if someone were ready to admit to lacking intelligence, should we expect that such a person would also emphasize the importance of being unintelligent? From this perspective, we begin to see that the positive end of the continuum is the one toward which individuals would gravitate, and thus, seen psychologically, this model is also likely to point more to the desired person—to the highly sociable, intelligent, tolerant person—as the self-knower.

WHERE IS THE PSYCHOLOGY?

The self-knower school as depicted above points regularly in the direction of a person whose attributes are highly desired within the realm of certain theorists or therapists. This realm, or culture, agrees largely on the attributes that the self-knower must possess. In all of this discussion, one tends to forget the psychology of the less desirable person, whose character may be summarized quite efficiently as the opposite of that of the supposed self-knower: The person would be inconsistent from setting to setting, and it would be difficult to find consistency between the person's words and actions. Such an individual would also be highly attuned to status hierarchies (thus respecting those who emanate power and not respecting the less powerful), and dependent on others in matters of morality. Thus, the central qualities of the self-knower portrait are simply turned around, and we have a nonautonomous, dependent, authoritarian, hypocritical, inconsistent person.

Is the self-knower school interested in this antiportrait? Certainly not in the sense that people would be advised to match their qualities to such a portrait. But indirectly, there is indeed such interest. Rogers (1961), for instance, observed that entities such as our anti-self-knower are created by a social atmosphere that does not foster the traits seen in the positive picture. He referred to factors that interfere with the natural development of the self-kernel. Rogers entertained such possibilities as an authoritarian upbringing, that is, too much direction for one's actions and too little decision freedom.

Similarly, Forisha (1981), who explored the background of feminist and less feminist women, referred the failure of emancipation to the suppressive forces of culture, and ascribed success to factors residing ultimately within the individual, such as self-awareness, learning one's "own needs" as opposed to the needs dictated by society, and learning to recognize one's own, true emotions, as opposed to the emotions taught by society.

The self-knower school is indeed interested in the negative portrait, but its interest is qualitatively very different from its interest in the positive portrait. All developments, traits, or behavioral syndromes that fall within the positive portrait are regarded as being born out of the innately given kernel of self—that is, the natural, core essence of the individual—and are pure indicators of the self-knower in that those characteristics cannot be traced back to societal influence. No further detail is given concerning other possible contributing factors. However, as soon as the individual begins to manifest aspects of the undesired image, the possession of those undesired features is ascribed to the environment as the sole source of the facadelike antiportrait. We are dealing, then, with theories that see the underpinnings of traits as residing in two very different locations; the choice of the location depends on whether the behavior to be explained is "positive" or "negative."

SOCIAL INFLUENCE AS A DESTRUCTIVE ELEMENT

The reasoning is similar in Kohlberg's system (1980) of lower and higher moralities. The morally "weakest" person is the one whose judgments about correct behavior and thinking are fully dependent on others. Such an individual's standards of correct moral functioning shift according to who is present to influence the individual. Thus, at the earlier stages, there is no consistency, no reliability, and the moral behaviors do not reflect the true, inner self. At the fourth stage, the person begins to implement values that have earlier been incorporated or internalized from social contexts, and the immediate presence of others is not necessary to the use of these internalized values. A certain autonomy is present at this stage.

Then the system goes a step further. In the transition to Stages 5 and 6, individuals distance themselves from all societal influence; Kohlberg wrote of a "self-generated" morality. At this point, the person has ceased to be influenced by the moral systems of society, by laws, or by constitutions, and develops an "original" morality.

The parallel to the self-knower school is direct: The highest level— that is, the level most valued by the theorist—is attained without ostensible outside influence. In Kohlberg's system, the highest moral principles are somehow generated creatively and individually; in the self-knowledge school, the behavioral potentials associated with the self-knower stem directly from the unique core of the person. Social influence, for Kohlberg, is associated with a weak morality; social influence for the self-knower school is associated with the non-self-knowing person.

The reader should note that the social factors referred to in the context of the non-self-knower cannot be identified or examined scientifically. "Social influence" is simply used to account for the existence of tendencies that run counter to the idealized picture of the self-knower.

The rejection of possible social bases of self-knowledge is highly explicit in several of the self-knower theories. Rogers (1961) wrote repeatedly of the role of therapy in assisting people to remove social facades, that is, hindrances to true self-knowledge. Similarly, the highest level of self-knowing in Maslow (1968) is "uncontrolled," "reflexlike," "instinctive," and "spontaneous," and thus seemingly impervious to any civilizing forces that society may try to impose.

In another work, Maslow (1977) expressed his dissatisfaction with social-feedback sources of self-feelings even more unambiguously. Citing Erich Fromm, Karen Horney, Ayn Rand, and Carl Rogers, he pointed to the danger of basing one's sense of self on feedback from others and recommended that self-feelings be drawn from one's "actual competence and fitness for the task at hand" (p. 88). The "actual self" is, then, an entity that the person must perceive directly. One's position in the social structure, or feedback and influence from the social milieu, can only interfere with the correctness of these "objective perceptions." The idea is that the human is—in some nonexplicable manner—equipped to perceive and acknowledge such central and true self-aspects. In case the reader is interested in knowing just how this all comes about, Maslow's answer (1977) is "willpower," "decisiveness," and "responsibility" (p. 88).

Forisha's (1981) analysis of femininity is similar. She described the course of therapy as one of differentiation between the self and others, enabling a woman to act on her true, internal facets and not on the social facade imposed from without. But what, concretely, brings about this recognition of the inner self? Little is said other than that it is necessary for the woman to push aside the socializing influences that tend to cover over the true, emancipated self. In short, any reader who would like to have a causal model of when and how the inner core is realized, and of exactly *what* is realized, will be frustrated. The whole process is ultimately traced back to the person's willingness, or willpower, regarding the readiness to reject social influences.

THE NONPSYCHOLOGICAL CHARACTER

Why have we charged that the systems depicted here, with perhaps the exception of Markus's notions, are not psychological? Let's see what they actually accomplish in assisting us to understand the psychology of the self and the psychology of self-knowledge.

Identifying the Self-Knower

The foremost impression one gains in reading through these works is that the theorists' focus is on the identification of the self-knowing person, that is, on the person as a unit, an entity that "knows itself." This is accomplished, as we have seen in all versions of the self-knower school, by setting up positively sanctioned criteria (consistency, spontaneity, and autonomy) that are said to reflect self-knowingness. But where is the psychology? Is a psychologist required for this task of identification?

Let us alter the task slightly: Instead of trying to identify the self-knower, it now becomes the theorist's task to identify the "spiritual" individual. One could then appeal both to the wisdom of the person on the street and to certain psychologists: Given that the task stays on the level of identification, the amateur or professional psychologist would generate a list of personal characteristics, such as "shows abiding faith in broad principles," "draws strength from higher forces," and "attends church."

How does the theorist know that the list is the correct one? In this procedure of identification, there is no particularly good way to go about the task aside from making certain arbitrary judgments, and the judgments would, of course, be based on cultural wisdom about what makes up a spiritual person.

On the other hand, our amateur or professional theorist could move one step beyond the mere identification task and argue that, if there are, indeed, certain qualities that constitute the spiritual person, we should be able to talk about the beginnings of those qualities. Do they lie in learning, in imitation, or in certain age-specific socialization practices? Although such a procedure seems eminently reasonable, it would not be allowed if we continue to abide by the reasoning of the self-knower school. Rather, the answer would be, "Spirituality lies in the true, inborn roots of the person's self; it must be discovered. Social influence can only muddy the picture and retard the natural ripening of true spirituality."

This is, then, one reason for our thinking that the self-knower school functions antipsychologically. A causal analysis of the traits of the self-knower is rejected totally. As soon as the reader has an idea about a possible external (social) contributor to creativity, autonomy, or tolerance, the self-knower school must argue that such external influences can lead only to a covering over of the true self.

Confusing the Self and Self-Knowledge

There is a second reason for our doubting the psychological depth of the self-knower school. When a theorist deals with the topics of the self and of self-knowledge, the reader or neutral observer expects that these two topics will be kept straight. If we look at the kinds of behavioral potentials that interest the self-knower school (autonomy, creativity, spontaneity, consistency), we see that the theorist's interest is in a certain set of behavioral directions. It doesn't matter whether we call these directions habits, potentials, or self-components, but obviously, a pressing issue should be the following: How does it happen that certain individuals come to manifest these tendencies? A question that can hardly be separated from the first one is: How do people come to manifest or incorporate the contrary tendencies, that is, dependence, intolerance, or authoritarianism?

These kinds of issues can be examined completely independently of the person's *knowledge* of the behavioral tendencies. However, the self-knower school does not take this route. Instead, a certain set of behavioral tendencies is said to emanate directly from the core of one's inner being, no particular causal analysis being necessary, and in turn, this socially valued set of tendencies is said to reflect self-knowledge. Accordingly, creative people have *knowledge* of their tendencies to be creative, by definition. But what about the noncreative types? They cannot be given credit for having knowledge of their lacking creativity. Similarly, do tolerant people, by definition, have knowledge of their tolerance? And do intolerant people, by definition, *not* know themselves in that they do not know their own intolerance? Not only is the valued individual (the self-knower), then, recognized as possessing the traits of which the theorist approves, but the package is made still more positive in that the positive person is accorded the status of a self-knower. In taking this final step, the self-knower school equates the presence of certain behavioral directions with knowledge of those directions. In turn, there is no possibility of studying the coming and going of self-knowledge independent of the presence of certain behavioral potentials.

THE METHODS OF IDENTIFICATION

At this point, we have a sense of the general direction of the self-knower school. But it needs to be made more concrete. If the primary task of the self-knower school is, indeed, identification, then we need to have a close look at the methods of identification. How is the self-knower (i.e., the person who is valued and sought in the eyes of the theorist) recognized concretely? Via overt characteristics, on the basis of education, or social caste, or performance? The next chapter will show that the self-knower school, perhaps by historical accident, has come to depend on the *self-report* method. We might presume that this historical accident has to do with the self-knower school's being intertwined in therapeutic theories and techniques, and so one should not be surprised that evaluation via self-reports is particularly emphasized. As it happens, however, this dominant approach to identifying the self-knower (i.e., the self-report method) is so fraught with difficulties that its bearing on a psychological state of self-knowledge is questionable. We will see what these problems look like in the next chapter.

CHAPTER 4

SELF-REPORTS

CAN THEY REFLECT "PURE" SELF-KNOWLEDGE?

The researcher, the therapist, or any other person who wants to recognize someone's self-knowledge must rely on some indication of self-knowledge. This point is obvious enough. What is not so easily decipherable is the kind of indicator that the researcher or therapist should use. For example, one might want to argue that people who have come a long way, by societal standards—those who are artistically or scientifically creative—are necessarily self-knowing people. To be sure, this is the kind of evidence that Maslow (1968) took as a sign that someone has come into contact with the deepest and truest potential of oneself.

But the Maslow approach is an exception, and in fact, even Maslow— as other members of the self-knower school—depended on verbal statements of the persons being studied or helped. What kinds of verbal statements? For one, statements about weaknesses, anxieties, or wrongdoings are characteristically taken as signs of having truly recognized something deep within one's personality: "I have a fear of strange people," "I have no self-confidence," "I am prejudiced against foreigners," or "I am very dependent on Persons X, Y, and Z." The admission of weakness is the central theme of Jourard's views (1971) about mental health. Only when deep (that is, intimate, negative) self-based statements are made can the therapist, researcher, observer, or other person be sure that the statements bear on self-knowledge. Thus, for Jourard, self-references that might otherwise be suppressed or forbidden in the presence of others are taken as a sign of direct and healthy contact with the inner core of the self.

The other representatives of the self-knowledge school have agreed with Jourard, although many other kinds of self-references have also been taken as signs of direct self-observation. For instance, it is thought to be normal, and a sign of progress in therapy, that the patient gradually begins to communicate signs of "growth" via self-references: "I can now accept my weaknesses better," "I feel stronger," "Finally, I understand why I have been insulting him," "I know myself better now," "I feel that I am autonomous," "I feel good about my values," or "I am relatively certain of my abilities."

ONLY WORDS, OR REPORTS OF SOMETHING?

Let us put forward a highly cynical proposition: One could imagine that all such self-observations as "I have a fear of cats" or "My self-confidence has improved" are, in fact, based in no way on internal psychological states, behavioral tendencies, or anything else about one's own person. That is, we can conceive of a case in which a person's verbal statements simply occur, perhaps because they have been practiced or shaped previously, because they are especially appropriate to the given social setting, or simply because the person is required to say something. In such cases, the verbiage would not have anything to do with one's actual internal state or condition. The extreme case would be a parrot that has lived in a psychotherapist's office and that has come to master such phrases as "I am feeling better about myself" and "I have low self-esteem."

The psychology of verbal behavior would not find these examples to be so farfetched. It has long been documented that self-references can be shaped directly by subtle reinforcers (Doob, 1947; Verplanck, 1955), and similarly, attitudes can also be shaped rapidly by reinforcement techniques (Berkowitz & Knurek, 1969; Insko & Oakes, 1966; Staats & Staats, 1958; Zanna, Kiesler, & Pilkonis, 1970). A child's saying, "That is a dog," is from this perspective not fundamentally different from the parrot's or the adult's saying, "I have low self-esteem," given that any verbal statement can have multiple determinants, many of which have nothing to do with stable internal aspects. Unfortunately, this simple and documentable observation is sometimes neglected, particularly when a person's statement carries an "I, me, or mine" character. The presence of the first-person pronoun misleads us into thinking that the statement bears directly on an inner condition of the person. But this is not necessarily so, and to be sure, there are some research findings that point toward the arbitrariness of assuming that "I" and "me" statements are grounded in introspection about something lurking inside oneself.

SELF-REPORTS STEMMING FROM SOCIAL DESIRABILITY

We shall continue working with the assumption that reports about one's inner condition can, in fact, be governed by events that are quite irrelevant to the internal features of oneself that one talks about. We are thus assuming that a person who says, "I fear strangers" or "I have won new self-confidence," may be saying such things *not* on the basis of looking inward directly, to one's fear level or self-confidence level, but instead on the basis of entirely different factors.

One such factor is the tendency to express oneself in a socially desirable way. According to Crowne and Marlowe (1960; 1964), individuals with a high general level of anxiety about disapproval are also highly prone to steering their behavior, and their verbal responses in particular, in the direction of the socially wished-for (Crowne, 1979, p. 183). The direction taken in research has centered, for the most part, on a scale of social desirability, developed by Crowne and Marlowe (1960). The persons with high anxiety about receiving disapproval, who on this scale show an express interest in abiding by the interests of others, can be shown to attend more to conformity pressures, are more defensive (in the sense of not owning up to weaknesses), and are inclined generally to avoid leaving a negative impression. Although Crowne and Marlowe themselves did not delve explicitly into introspective or self-disclosing verbiage as reflecting the influence of social desirability, such an analysis would seem rather easy, given the general social desirability principle. An example is found in a study by Cravens (1975).

The setting created by Cravens entailed female subjects' discussing dating behavior. They were asked to describe to a second woman what kind of man they would enjoy dating on a steady basis. This format obviously gave the participants an opportunity to reveal their deepest feelings about their relationships with men, their strengths and weaknesses interpersonally, their sexual inadequacies, and the like. To be sure, Cravens's main interest was in the intimacy of self-disclosures.

Cravens placed subjects either in a "private" condition, in which they expected no publicity for their remarks, or in a "public" condition, where the subjects learned that their remarks might be further publicized in a classroom or even in scientific publications. This latter condition interests us especially, as it is here that the subjects' level of social desirability should make a difference.

The way in which each female subject spoke with the second woman was then analyzed for the depth or intimacy of the disclosures. Such comments as "I like a guy to be enjoyable" were scored as nondisclosing, in that there was no revealing of detailed personal information. At the other end of the continuum, such remarks as "I have trouble dating guys that are my own age" were regarded as high in self-disclosure, on the grounds of their ostensibly communicating affects, needs, or fantasies. True to expectation, the subjects who scored high on the social-desirability measure evidenced significantly more disclosing of intimate self-related aspects, but only when the setting was cast as highly public. If no publicity was expected, the subjects with a high tendency toward social desirability were actually *less* intimate in their self-related remarks.

The implication of these findings is explicit enough: Just because a certain set of remarks *sounds* introspective and attuned to important affects does not mean that those remarks are, in fact, based on direct insight into psychological events. The simple combination of expected publicity and a readiness to please others (high social desirability) would seem to be sufficient to push subjects to create the impression of having told deep truths about themselves.

On the other hand, it may be that the subjects with high-social-desirability tendencies also happen to possess more intimate details to share with others. That is, people who are intent on making a favorable impression may have experienced more in the way of intimate relationships, or more disappointments, or the like. Fine. The study does not rule this alternative out at first glance. On the other hand, why should the high "social desirables" tell the truth about themselves only in the public conditions? If there is an automatic readiness to introspect and to report on those introspections, then privacy should not inhibit truth telling. If we put all of the results together, it looks much more as if the high socially desirable participants were strongly affected by the public conditions. The larger and more significant the anticipated audience, the more they talked about what was implicitly expected of them.

SELF-REPORTS STEMMING FROM STATUS RELATIONS

An empirical work by Brooks (1974) also looked at the intimacy of self-disclosures, and again, this study questioned whether the depth of self-related remarks is governed directly by a process of introspection. Two aspects of the study are interesting for our theme here:

1. For some subjects the interviewer was of the same sex, and for others, the interviewer was of the opposite sex. This variation

made a considerable difference for both male and female subjects, in that the subjects disclosed more deeply to a different-sex interviewer.

2. Brooks also varied the status of the interviewer: In the high-status case, the interviewer was cast as one of the youngest, and yet most experienced counselors at the university counseling center, whereas in the low-status condition, the subjects thought that the interviewer was a student, currently engaged in training in counseling students. The men responded to high status by saying more intimate things about themselves, and curiously, the opposite prevailed among the female subjects; that is, the disclosures were more intimate when the interviewer was billed as a low-status person.

The exact psychological interpretation of these differences between male and female respondents remains an open question, but the important lesson for the present is that the observer (interviewer or therapist) gains a different "truth" about an individual as a function of the power relations and other social constellations of the setting.

To summarize the above, the self-knower school depends heavily on people's reports about themselves. Judgments about self-knowledge or insight, weaknesses and strength, progress or problems, are generally made on the basis of the respondent's verbal statements. The purpose of this section has been to show that self-directed remarks, no matter how "deep," "introspective," or "I"-related they may sound, can have very simple determinants. Among these determinants are such general factors as the person's readiness to present a socially desirable picture. Thus, if the social context encourages a high level of confession, intimate-sounding comments, and the like, the person wanting to avoid disapproval is apt to generate such intimacies, particularly if the recipients can approve or disapprove of the person. Given that such intimate self-revelations can be controlled by the person's social desirability level, we are led to be skeptical about the introspective value of these revelations. It is entirely possible that such self-directed remarks are not at all based on the person's psychological states or conditions but are shaped entirely by the social setting plus the need to make oneself acceptable within that setting.

ACTIVE AVOIDANCE OF SELF-CONFRONTATION

Part of the assumption of the self-knowledge schools relates to the person's general willingness to open up. In an ideal world, the individual who has a problem, and who simultaneously is induced to focus on the self, should be inclined to admit to that problem—to try to open up in the interest of solving the problem. Therefore, if we continue with the theme of intimate revelations and disclosures of problems and weaknesses, these would ideally be seen most frequently among individuals who (1) possess a salient weakness and (2) are particularly focused on themselves, and thus on that weakness. Unfortunately for this ideal portrait of the human, something resembling the opposite can be found in the relevant empirical work.

In an experiment by Duval, Wicklund, and Fine (in Duval & Wicklund, 1972), there were two main groups of subjects: those who experienced positive feedback about their creativity and intelligence, and those who experienced negative feedback. Thus the stage was set for subjects who had received unfavorable feedback to confront themselves regarding the weakness implied by the feedback. Each subject was then asked to wait in a small room alone but was allowed to leave after several minutes (the exact time spent in the room was completely up to the subject). For some of the subjects, there was a mirror in the small waiting room, forcing their attention on themselves. For other subjects, there was only a wall, and no mirror. The interesting issue was the length of time that the subjects stayed in the small waiting room, and in fact, they generally waited about eight minutes. However, one group of subjects proved to be an exception: the subjects who (1) had experienced negative feedback about their creativity and intelligence and (2) were confronted with their mirror images in the small waiting room. They waited on the average only six minutes.

What does this experiment demonstrate? When a personal shortcoming is salient (faltering creativity and intelligence) and particularly when conditions are conducive to self-confrontation (the presence of a mirror), there is a pronounced tendency to avoid the situation. Thus, rather than "taking advantage of the setting" to work through one's problem, or to "come to terms" with the salient negative feedback, the subject's reaction is flight. On the basis of these effects, we would also expect fewer intimate revelations from such subjects, and this is the topic of a study by Archer, Hormuth, and Berg (1982).

In the study by Archer et al., the subjects were placed in a context in which self-disclosures were called for. In one condition (of particular interest here), there was pressure to engage in deep, intimate self-descriptions. The subjects undertook their self-disclosures either in the presence of a mirror or not. The mirror had the effect of suppressing intimacy, so that the subjects who were not confronted with their own mirror images evidenced the deepest, most intimate disclosures.

This result makes a very useful point in our evaluation of the self-knowledge school. The self-knower—thus, the person who readily, freely, and voluntarily discusses personal problems—is an internal contradiction. By definition (within the self-knower school), a self-knower is a person who can recognize problems—introspect about them—and then communicate these faults and other intimacies to others. And also by definition, the self-knower is a person who is self-aware and who welcomes self-confrontation (cf. Gur & Sackeim, 1979). But such definitions of the self-knower are internally incongruous. The very person who has salient problems, and who is in a setting that promotes self-confrontation, is the same person who *shirks* intimate self-disclosures.

AVOIDANCE AND SOCIAL DESIRABILITY

The study by Cravens, which we summarized above, indicates that a chronic tendency toward social desirability produces a certain "cooperativeness" in settings where intimate self-disclosures are appropriate. These results manifest the general thrust of the social desirability notion, which is that the person with such inclinations tries to appear proper and aboveboard and does not like to create a flawed impression. Using this same logic, one can also imagine that the person with high social desirability does not like to leave a lasting impression of being psychologically unsound.

Carrying this possibility into the clinical setting, Strickland and Crowne (1963) measured the social desirability scores of patients in an outpatient psychiatric clinic and obtained the following results. They found a decided tendency for highly socially desirable patients to terminate therapy comparatively early. They were approximately twice as likely as the low socially desirable patients to terminate therapy after about 20 hours. Does this simply mean that the "highs" were less in need of therapy? A further data point, collected directly from these patients' therapists, offers quite a different interpretation. The therapists judged the high-social-desirability group to be particularly defensive; in fact, the correlation between defensiveness ratings and social desirability was a very high .67. This finding fits the picture of the highly socially desirable person quite nicely; the basis of the social desirability scale is a defensive posture with regard to threats to one's self-worth.

What is the lesson for the present? The high-social-desirability person is not a good patient, that is, is unwilling over the long run to delve into threatening personal problems, at least in a clinical setting. Perhaps the reader can appreciate this result even more by taking note of one of the items of the social desirability scale: "I'm always willing to admit it when I make a mistake" (a "yes" answer increases one's social desirability score).

SELF-REPORTS AS COMPENSATION:
REALITY TURNED BACKWARD

A curious omission among the self-knower theories is the primary thesis of Adler (1912). Inferiority feelings and striving for superiority are, in Adler's theory, the elements of a process that turns the validity of self-reports completely on its head. Adler's starting point was any rudimentary inferiority (physical or psychological defect). It is then a simple jump to the assumption that people with pronounced inferiorities establish the goal of overcoming those deficits. A person of slight build would compensate by engaging in athletics, someone who is intellectually ungifted would pursue philosophy, and the like.

Adler's basic principle of compensation finds a systematic and also an empirical treatment in a more recent formulation, called *symbolic self-completion* (Wicklund & Gollwitzer, 1982). Here, the compensation idea has been made more specific, and in particular, the starting point is the individual who is committed to excellence in a particular endeavor, such as basketball, music, foreign languages, business, or any other pursuit, whether occupational or not. Once the person realizes shortcomings in that area, such as lack of experience, poor quality of education, or faltering performance, there is said to be a tendency to acquire new symbols of excellence in that area. Among other possibilities, one route to self-symbolizing consists of gaining recognition for one's competence via self-descriptions. Simply stated, if a person is objectively inadequate in an area that is of high personal importance, then self-descriptions can be expected to be exaggerated upward.

We can begin with a study by Gollwitzer and Wicklund (1985), in which all of the participants (all males) were firmly committed to being good in athletics, or journalism, or some other undertaking. Thus, every participant had an area of specialty. Half the subjects were then given reason to be uncertain about their potential in that special area in that they were given personality feedback, showing them that their own personality profiles were quite discrepant from the profiles of experts in that same area. For instance, the subject whose specialty was journalism was asked to fill out a personality questionnaire and was then shown the personality-questionnaire responses (i.e., profile) of an alleged expert. It was apparent to the subject that his own profile was substantially discrepant from that of the expert. The other subjects were given no such uncertainty induction.

Subsequently, all the subjects were asked to describe themselves to an attractive woman. Among other questions that formed the basis of their self-descriptions, they were asked for their percentile standing in their own area (e.g., journalism) relative to that of other students. On the average, the subjects who were not given the uncertainty-creating manipulation indicated that they were superior to 57% of the other students. And interestingly, among the subjects who received the discrepant personality feedback, this figure was 73%. The greater the objective basis for being uncertain about one's abilities, the more favorable the self-estimate.

This effect was even more pronounced when the woman created pressure on the subject to be self-deprecating. In one set of conditions, it was communicated to the subject that the woman was especially fond of self-deprecating, or modest, men. Confronted with this cue, the subjects who had not received the discrepant personality feedback responded directly to her wishes, indicating a percentile level of 43%. In contrast, the males who had been told that their personalities were unsuitable to their pursuits described themselves at the level of better than 66% of the other students.

If we move back a step from the theoretical purpose of this experiment and ask ourselves, "What does the study tell us about self-knowledge?" we see a very clear point. If a person shows a strong interest in a particular area, no matter whether in athletic, intellectual, social, or artistic realms, a realistic self-knowledge would entail reporting strengths and weaknesses to the degree that there is objective evidence of them. If the person has a poor education, self-knowledge must mean that this weakness will be acknowledged. And if the person experiences feedback indicating a weak potential on the basis of personality information, this weakness should also be reported. But what actually happens? Weakness is transformed into apparent strength via the self-report; those whose personalities are discrepant from the ideal personality claim to be much superior to the average student.

It is often the case that self-knowledge issues arise when an area is important to someone. One example lies within psychotherapy, where there is no doubt that areas to which people are highly committed can eventually create problems. What should happen, then, when the self-report is trusted as an indicator of self-knowledge, especially in important areas in which the person is faltering? The self-report is apt to be a covering over of weaknesses, and the observer who trusts the self-report as a direct reflection of an internal psychological condition is making a serious blunder, no matter whether the observer is a research psychologist or a therapist. The statement "I feel adequate as an intellectual" or "My relations with members of the opposite sex are one of my strong points" can quite easily represent nothing more than a simple compensation for a faulty, insecure intellectual capacity, or for chronic problems in getting along with members of the opposite sex.

The obverse should also hold: Modesty or self-deprecation in an area

of high personal importance may be a sign of underlying, objective security. This latter point is underscored in experiments by Wicklund and
Gollwitzer (1981) and Gollwitzer, Wicklund, and Hilton (1982), in which
subjects were asked to feign weaknesses. The subjects who had a relatively
high basis for objective security within their areas of specialty were more
willing to engage in self-deprecation for the benefit of another person.
However, those whose objective security was questionable could not
readily bring themselves to be self-deprecating.

We emphasize the above point because it is occasionally maintained
that something like the opposite is the case, that is, that people who are
especially attached to an area have deeper self-knowledge in that area. A
passage from Markus (1983) represents this point of view:

> In self-relevant domains, however, such mindlessness or ignorance is unlikely
> to be the case. In these areas, individuals will often be significantly aware of
> many of the antecedents and consequences of their behavior. The effective
> administrator can confidently describe how and why he performed in a par-
> ticular manner. . . . The behavior . . . will be systematically related to what these
> individuals know about themselves and to what they report they know. (p. 546)

If we extrapolate from this comment, it follows that the *in*effective admin-
istrator should also be able to offer deep and accurate self-descriptions. But
the research simply contradicts this point of view: If a person is committed
to an area (i.e., if the activities are highly self-relevant), there is much more
reason to think that self-descriptions are guided by compensation.

The literature on self-handicapping (Frankel & Snyder, 1978; Jones &
Berglas, 1978) and excuse making (Snyder, 1990; Snyder & Higgins, 1988)
is also in direct conflict with the idea that involvement in an area is
associated with a more objective self-evaluation in that area. Excuse making is particularly likely to manifest itself when people are highly involved
in a performance realm and when their esteem in that same realm has been
threatened. Excuse making, which entails locating the cause for one's
performance outside one's own person, is, of course, contrary to an objective or fair analysis of one's own actions.

BUT THE SELF-KNOWER "DOES NOT COMPENSATE"

The protest to the above point, if an objection were to come from the
self-knower school, would be that only the immature, non-self-knowing
individual would compensate. Compensation belongs to the family of
social facades that are implemented by the non-self-knower, and once the
person has had self-insight, such facadelike mechanisms will no longer
prevail. But how does the researcher or therapist know that an individual

is a self-knower? The route is exclusively through self-descriptions, and as we have tried to demonstrate, the self-description as a direct route to the inner psychological condition of the person is flawed. Rogers's person (1961) who has come to "express more self-confidence" may just as well be the person whose self-confidence is, in fact, at a particularly low level; Maslow's "self-knower," manifesting feelings (i.e., self-descriptions) of energy and competence, can just as easily be an incompetent, floundering person. And finally, subjects who score high on scales such as Warshaw and Davis's "self-understanding" instrument (1984) may well be individuals whose sense of their own behavioral dispositions is not secure. Their findings of a curvilinear relationship between claimed self-knowledge and consistency in self-reported behavior would support such a supposition.

HOW CAN ACCURACY IN SELF-DESCRIPTIONS COME ABOUT?

Quite independent of the self-knowledge school of thought, there has recently been a good deal of discussion about the extent to which people are capable of understanding or tracing their own psychological processes. The center of these discussions is an article by Nisbett and Wilson (1977b), and we can best depict their point of view by way of an example. Subjects were asked to perform a task, either in the presence of an ostensibly disturbing noise or else without the noise. In fact, the obtrusive noise had no actual detrimental effects on task performance, but on the subjective side, the subjects were quite certain that the noise affected their performance adversely.

The effects pointed to by Nisbett and Wilson are usually of this nature: A given stimulus configuration has an effect (or sometimes no effect) on subjects' behavior or thinking, and the subjects are very frequently wrong about their estimate of the impact of the stimulus. In this sense, humans can be shown to possess quite limited self-knowledge; that is, people are rather unclear about whether their behaviors have been affected by certain stimulus patterns.

Can one extend this thesis slightly, to argue that people have no general access to their dispositions, values, and attitudes or, more generally, to their behavioral potentials? The recent literature is well on the side of a critical stance. A number of overviews have demonstrated that self-reports of behavioral potentials (attitudes, values, and personality traits) seldom have much to do with the behaviors that are supposed to stem from those self-reports (see Gibbons, 1983; Mischel, 1968; Wicker, 1969; Wicklund, 1982). It is not uncommon to find that the relation between an attitude toward an object and actual behavior toward that object is zero (Wicker, 1969). For instance, it can readily be shown that the relationship between attitudes toward punishment and actual willingness to use punishment is about zero (cf. Carver, 1975). Thus, one may well want to extend the statement of Nisbett and Wilson to include all kinds of behavioral potentials, and not just knowledge about one's reaction to overt stimuli. It appears to be the case that people generally are not in a position to introspect accurately about their attitudes or other behavioral potentials.

On the other hand, a kind of psychology of self-reports has developed within recent years, a psychology that deals with the events that need to take place in order that a self-report have some bearing on a person's actual behavioral readiness. We will mention three of these developments here:

1. One technique involves appealing to self-reporting on extremes. Willerman, Turner, and Peterson (1976) found that requesting subjects to indicate *how extremely* they could imagine behaving, rather than how they *typically* behave, served as a considerably more accurate predictor of actual behavior.

2. Having a clear or recent behavior base from which to judge one's dispositions has a marked beneficial effect on the accuracy of self-reports of those dispositions (Fazio & Zanna, 1978; Zanna & Fazio, 1982). The idea here is that asking a person, outside the behavioral context, for an attitude or other disposition does not allow the person to put the answer into a behaviorally relevant context. However, if the person first has a chance to behave in some relevant way, and then to report the attitude, the statement of attitude (self-report) is then a considerably better predictor of future behaviors.

3. Another approach to self-report accuracy was implemented by Pryor, Gibbons, Wicklund, Fazio, and Hood (1977), drawing on a theory of self-awareness (Duval & Wicklund, 1972; see Gibbons, 1990, for an overview). The idea here is that potential discrepancies between self-reports and usual behavior levels are scarcely realized when the person is not in a self-aware state. And thus, when persons look into a mirror or hear their own tape-recorded voices, self-reports occurring shortly after such inductions have a much closer relation to behavior (see also Hormuth, 1982; Scheier, Buss, & Buss, 1978).

These three approaches lend a sense of optimism to the idea that there can be self-knowledge in the sense of accurate reporting of one's own behavioral dispositions. But in order for self-reports to function, the researcher must be aware of the processes that guide them. If one is content to assume that all verbal reflections and so-called introspections stem directly from an inner psychological state, the resulting self-report will be nothing more than a jumbled product of remarks steered by social desirability, by other situational pressures, or by compensation. And this is the primary difficulty with the self-knower school. No attention is given to psychological factors underlying the direction taken in self-reports, because the individual is given credit for knowing the inner self simply by "wanting to."

SELF-KNOWLEDGE INDEPENDENT OF LANGUAGE?

One can assume for a moment, however erroneously, that people are generally capable of looking inside, directly at their behavioral potentials, and that they are capable of recognizing what they then sense or perceive. There is still a leap to the accurate self-report: it has to be formulated in some communicable language. And as it turns out, humans do not have access to a universal language of inner states or dispositions. This idea is illustrated in research on children by Benenson and Dweck (1986) and Miller (1984). At about the age of 7, children are not yet linguistically equipped to speak about success and failures (neither their own nor others') in personality-trait terms or even simple dispositional terms. These modes of expression apear to become familiar to children after the age of 9 or 10, according to a careful study by Benenson and Dweck (1986). Furthermore, and independent of age, there are societies in which the use of trait terms to account for behavior is rather low in comparison to their use in such Western countries as the United States (see Miller, 1984). Were one to try to analyze the prevalence of self-knowledge in Third World societies by looking at trait references, the results would be surprising for many psychologists, because the trait repertoire (which is a large part of the Western "self-knowledge" repertoire) would be somewhat lacking.

The self-knowledge approach of Markus (1977, 1983) is an interesting case in point here. Her respondents were regarded as being self-knowing when they said that a given trait dimension was important to them and when they were extreme in their self-ratings. But what would self-knowledge consist of among a sample of young children, or among a sample of respondents from a society in which traitlike terms are not a central aspect of discourse? We do not need to belabor the point: There could not be any self-knowledge in the sense of the self-knower school because the self-description approach to defining self-knowledge is completely dependent on respondents' verbal skills with trait terms, that is, words having to do with behavioral potential, capacities, or feelings.

The case is no different for other sectors of the self-knower school. Those who communicate openly and freely about themselves will appear to "know" themselves deeply only insofar as they choose numerous trait terms in characterizing themselves. People who simply describe their work and play activities, or their likes and dislikes, would not be seen as having deeper insight into the kernel of the self. This much is explicit in a commentary on aspects of clinical psychology by Ortlieb (1973), who concluded that patients are pronounced as "healthy" to the extent that their self-descriptions use the psychological language that is favored by the therapist.

It would therefore not be correct to say that the person simply experiences attitudes, feelings, emotions, or other potentials and then reports them with the help of the available language tools. Rather, the character of what is perceived is shaped considerably by the immediate environment. The work of Zillmann (1978), derived from the thinking of Schachter (1964), makes it clear that such experiences as "sexual excitement" or "aggressive feelings" are not simple products of introspection: instead, they are highly dependent on social cues provided in settings in which the person becomes physiologically aroused. States of physiological arousal are sufficiently vague so that different interpretations can be attached to them, and the apparent "self-knower" will report very different kinds of emotions, depending on the context in which the arousal is experienced. Whether a case of physiological excitement is interpreted as being the effect of physical exercise or as sexual arousal depends largely on the information in the immediate context (Zillmann, 1978).

Thus, we see numerous problems in the self-knower school's total reliance on self-reports as evidence of self-knowledge. Social desirability and other social pressures are often the primary determinants of certain self-reports; the need to prove oneself worthy in important areas can twist self-reports into compensatory devices; the use of self-reports is possible only to the degree that the person has incorporated a self-report "language" that is acceptable to the receiver; and finally, self-reports about an inner process, such as physiological arousal, may be greatly colored by the available social cues. On the other hand, many kinds of self-reports (i.e., those regarding behavioral potential) can indeed be accurate, but the conditions prerequisite to this accuracy must be established, and they depend, in turn, on the researcher's willingness to allow that self-reports are guided by changing psychological variables, not solely and automatically by the static internal condition of the organism.

SELF-KNOWLEDGE INDEPENDENT OF CULTURE AND HISTORY?

The lesson of developmental psychology and the intercultural work of Miller (1984) is a simple one: The language of self-knowledge is not universal. And perhaps even more dramatic than the language issue is the fact that the individual—as a self-unit, as a self-contained, verbalizable personality—is also not universal across generations and across epochs. When we examine Baumeister (1986), Elias (1969), Sennett (1974), or Weber (1920), we discover that the strong consciousness of the individual personality—the person as a self-unit—is a relatively recent phenomenon. One thesis has it that the necessity of complex human interactions, particularly in modern cities, brings forth the necessity of the individual's being identifiable and of manifesting a personality (see Sennett, 1974). In contrast, when social roles are dominant in defining everyday goings-on, so that social functions dominate the manner in which individuals interact, then the uniqueness and personality of each person are not so crucial.

Sennett's primary distinction (1974) is between actions in the public sphere and those in the private sphere. He described at great length what the public sphere meant, for instance, in 18th-century London and Paris, where public behavior consisted largely of socially defined roles and where costumes and gestures accentuated the workings of these roles. By his account, people went about their public functions and exercised their competencies without exposing their private selves, thus without dwelling on their own and others' personalities. In more modern society, according to Sennett's observations, public settings have been transformed into occasions for displaying and disclosing one's "authentic" self. Sennett discussed the modern phenomenon of intimacy in public places, meaning the tendency to exchange self-disclosures with others, and noted that, when two people proceed to play the mutual-disclosure game, they reach a point at which their private repertoires have been spent. The relationship then dissolves into boredom.

By Sennett's account, there is a constant pressure in modern societies toward the functioning person's not merely serving a suitable public function, but also displaying authenticity and genuineness (i.e., "much personality") simultaneously. This is ostensibly true in politics as well as in the performing arts. The intimacy of the performer's personality has become more central than the performance itself. Thus, public behavior (the role or the actual performance) has been replaced by the display of the performer's authentic personality.

Casting a negative glance at the modern, self-disclosing society, Sennett characterized a civilized interaction as one in which the players wear masks, whereas the uncivilized interaction disposes of the masks; the players plague one another with their concerns about their true and real selves, at the same time being ultimately interested in the other's true self.

In a somewhat comparable analysis by Baumeister (1986), the modern instability of social institutions such as religion, moral systems, roles, and classes makes the concept of an individual self, or "unique personality," necessary:

> Society—both the general society at large and the specific family and social world of the individual—thus forms a rather incomplete context for identity today. The concept of the inner self has expanded over the recent centuries. The inner self is considered large, stable and continuous, unique, vitally important, real, and difficult to know. (p. 265)

The idea that the self and consciousness of one's individuality are products of societal necessities is, of course, foreign to the basic premises of the self-knower school. Predicating mental health on the discovering of one's authentic self assumes implicitly that some such authentic unit has always existed in the individual, across time, across generations, and, of course, that the presence of this kernel is culture-free. However, if we were to reverse the trends of the last 200–300 years and return to a societal condition in which one's integration into the group defines one's modes of behaving toward others, especially in the public realm, there would be little discussion of seeing or possessing authentic personalities. Not only would the language repertoire appropriate to individual personalities be lacking, but the idea of pursuing the true self would simply not be a significant concept among culturally defined ideas.

CHAPTER 5

THE THERAPIST
AND THE RESEARCHER

WHEN CONTROL NEEDS DETERMINE
THE ASCRIPTION OF SELF-KNOWLEDGE

The previous chapter was devoted to the self-reports of those who ostensibly have self-knowledge. Our focus was on the research subject or the patient or the observed person in general. And we tried to demonstrate how different psychological events taking place within the "self-knower" can influence self-reports in such a way that the person appears to others to be insightful, mature, or self-knowing.

This chapter turns the focus around and examines the observer, that is, the person who has an interest in knowing whether another is insightful, particularly the therapist and the researcher.

An overriding premise, that all observers are fair and objective perceivers of others, will become our antipremise in the course of this chapter. Many observers will maintain that they are fair-minded, objective, and unbiased in their perceptions of others, but we shall take a skeptical stance toward these kinds of assumptions. Perhaps a simple example will illustrate what we have in mind here.

It is not uncommon to encounter the assumption that certain kinds of training in the perceiving of others, particularly clinical training, have the effect of the observer's (in this case, the clinician's) coming to push aside biases with regard to others. The effect, so one may claim, is a balanced view of others, a good sense of the objective bases of others' verbal behaviors, and a sufficient overview of the course of influence between therapist and patient.

If a patient is judged to have improved with respect to a given anxiety, depression, or even addiction, it is assumed that the observer-clinician is making an objective judgment, grounded in actual symptoms. Similarly, if the therapist judges the patient to have gained in self-insight, autonomy, self-knowledge, and the like, it is readily assumed that these perceptions are grounded in objective fact. But let us have a brief glance at another point of view.

If a clinician has even a minimal basis for making a judgment about pathology, the pathology hypothesis is then formed, and subsequent perceptions are then molded into this hypothesis (Salovey & Turk, 1991). For instance, in studies by Langer and Abelson (1974) and Temerlin (1968), clinicians of different persuasions were, in some experimental conditions, given the hypothesis or expectation that a particular stimulus person was psychotic, already receiving treatment, and so on. Then, the clinicians were to evaluate that person on the basis of a tape. To be sure, the built-in expectation affected evaluations of the target persons markedly, and in the Langer and Abelson study, this effect was much more pronounced for psychodynamically oriented clinicians than for behaviorists. In short, the observer is not necessarily in a position to judge someone's symptoms objectively on the basis of a taped interview or some other behavioral sample. Prior expectations about the person's psychological condition color the evaluation of behavior substantially.

A parallel phenomenon was reported by Luborsky, Crits-Christoph, Mintz, and Auerbach (1988). In their own research, they observed that therapists' positive expectations with respect to the outcome of therapy had, in fact, a positive relation to subsequent independently judged success. As explanations of this seemingly stable phenomenon, Luborsky *et al.* suggested two possibilities. First, it may be that the therapist can indeed make an accurate prognosis, and second, the therapist could be part of a chain of events that results in a self-fulfilling prophecy (p. 295).

In still another commentary on clinical phenomena, one that brings us closer to the control theme of this chapter, Ortlieb (1973) charged that the clinician's perceptions of the patient's success in therapy are founded on a certain confusion. That is, if patients can learn to express themselves in the clinical-theoretical language of the therapist and can in turn apply that language to themselves, the therapist may be led into thinking that the patient is making actual progress. Ortlieb maintained that the therapist, who represents a powerful system and is also a prestige figure, is in a position to bring patients to express themselves in the clinically "appropriate" manner, in the terminology that has been learned in the therapeutic setting.

Ortlieb furthered his argument by reference to social learning theory (Bandura, 1965, 1969a, b; Bandura & Walters, 1963), observing that those persons whose contact is closest to another individual have the greatest extent of control over that individual. In the language of therapy, the closeness between patient and therapist is highest when the therapist possesses qualities that guarantee a positive relationship between both parties. In the Pennsylvania psychotherapy project of Luborsky *et al.* (1988), it was found that this therapist quality—closeness to the patient— is the best predictor of a favorable therapy outcome. Again, there is good reason to think that interpersonal facets of the therapy relationship—in this case, an element called *closeness*—set in motion a control-outcome effect.

Not only the therapist's choice of terminology, but also more primitive elements such as race or social class can affect the ultimate impression that therapists gain of their patients. A field study by Carkhuff and Pierce (1967) focused on four lay counselors, each of whom had completed a mental-health training program. The four of them had been evaluated in terms of prior training and effectiveness, to ensure that there were no appreciable differences among them. They did, however, differ in both social class and race: All combinations of upper and lower class and black and white were represented among the four therapists.

Each of the therapists undertook therapy sessions with a number of patients, and based on recordings of these sessions, independent raters evaluated the depth of self-exploration that was shown among the individual patients. Because depth of self-exploration is commonly regarded as an accompaniment of successful therapy, and of course as a sign of self-knowledge (e.g., Jourard's self-knowledge conception), the successful therapist should be the one who produces more of these self-focused explorations, defined as "actively and spontaneously engages in an inward probing to newly discover feelings or experiences about himself and his world" (Carkhuff & Pierce, 1967, p. 633).

A total of 16 patients was involved in the study, all with prior diagnoses of schizophrenia. This was a decidedly small sample, but the study was arranged so that each therapist saw each patient. The subsequent independent ratings of self-exploration were quite dramatic: there were very striking similarity effects, so that patients who stemmed from the same social class as their therapists showed more self-exploration (in the presence of that therapist), and patients whose race was the same as that of their therapists also showed more self-exploration (in the presence of that therapist).

It is not clear whether these effects were mediated by liking or dis-liking, by communication difficulties across class and race, or by other factors associated with the race and class variables. The important point is that success in therapy—in this case, operationalized by the frequency and depth of self-related remarks—seems to have a high dependence on the seemingly trivial factors of skin color and social background. The more similar the therapist–patient pair, the more power the therapist has to bring the patient to verbalize "healthy" indicators. The indicator in this case is the one pointed to by the self-knower school: self-related verbiage. Carkhuff and Pierce (1967) did not ask the therapists to evaluate their patients' degree of self-knowledge, or maturity, or progress, but one can be rather sure that such judgments would have been in line with the extent of self-exploration remarks, that is, congruent with patients' verbal co-operativeness.

CONVERGENCE OF BELIEFS AND EFFECTIVENESS OF THERAPY

As documented by Pepinsky and Karst (1964), convergence in social situations is a classic, long-observed phenomenon; one can point to the experiments of Sherif (1936) and Asch (1952) or to any number of more recent findings. A discrepancy between two sets of attitudes, values, styles, terminologies, or other communicable entities can quickly result in within-group pressure toward uniformity (for a theoretical analysis, see Festinger, 1950, 1954). Further, the uniformity is commonly drawn in the direction of the dominant force within the group, thus toward the expert, the prestige figure, the therapist, that is, the person who is informed or has prestige.

Thus, that convergence occurs within the therapeutic setting should not come as a great surprise, and to be sure, several therapeutic schools refer explicitly to convergence or influence phenomena. Frank (1959), for instance, even regarded therapy as "indoctrination." The interesting facet of convergence during the course of therapy is the relation between con-vergence and ostensible therapeutic progress. To be sure, there is a body of literature pertinent to this problem, and a summary statement by Beut-ler (1981) shows that convergence is reliably associated with rated im-provement in the client. The 16 studies reviewed by Beutler differed not only in term of the basis for converging (e.g., political or sexual attitudes; the value placed on therapy), but also in terms of the criterion of patient improvement; in the words of Beutler, "The observed relationship appears particularly strong when the criterion of improvement is the therapist's rating" (p. 82). In general, the criteria of improvement are based on patients' own ratings of their improvement, the therapist's judgment, or (rarely) an independent source of judgment, such as independent judges' evaluations. Before we get into the relevance of this phenomenon to the topic of control, it will be useful to take a closer look at a few examples of this direction of research.

CONVERGENCE IN KUDER PREFERENCE SCORES

Persons and Pepinsky (1966) conducted a study that involved five psychotherapists, two psychologists, and three social workers. The patients were 82 boys incarcerated in a state reformatory. The patients received both group therapy and individual therapy, always conducted by one particular therapist; characteristically, each therapist was responsible for about seven boys.

Therapeutic success was subsequently evaluated on the basis of psychological test scores and through behavioral observations, and the authors reported that 30 of the boys could be regarded as having been treated successfully. The important aspect is the degree of convergence associated with this success, and in this case, the authors examined the Kuder vocational interest profiles of the therapists and the patients: To what extent did the patients come to adopt the vocational interest patterns of their respective therapists? Interestingly, 67% of the successful group showed changes in Kuder scores in the direction of their therapists' scores, whereas only *two* of the unsuccessfully treated boys showed such a converging change.

Is change in the Kuder score part and parcel of successful psychotherapy? In the words of the authors, "Clients may model themselves after certain aspects of the therapist's behavior that are totally irrelevant to improvement" (p. 333). Thus, the question now is: Why is therapy more successful when patients allow themselves to be influenced by the therapist, even along lines that are seemingly irrelevant to treatment? Two further studies take us toward an answer.

CONVERGENCE IN MORAL VALUES

An oft-cited study by Rosenthal (1955) employed 12 patients with various psychoneurotic, personality, psychophysiological, and adjustment disorders. At the outset of treatment, the patients, as well as their therapists, filled out a moral values questionnaire that dealt with six aspects of sexuality, aggressiveness, discipline, and tolerance (e.g., "Masturbation is a sin"; "Capital punishment is wrong."). At the end of treatment, the patients filled out the scales once again. In addition, the relative success of the therapy was determined via an interview with the patient, conducted by Rosenthal himself, based on such questions as:

How did the patient feel as compared to when he began therapy?
If he felt better, how was he better?
How did he feel about his therapist?
How did he feel about therapy, terminating therapy, the future?
(Rosenthal, 1955, p. 432)

The reader will note that the results of these interviews, which were later coded by three judges and used as the improvement index, stemmed totally from the patients' subjective interpretation of the therapy and also depended on what the patients were willing to share with the author of the study. If the sessions had been mutually pleasant for therapist and patient, it is likely that the interview would have a positive ring. If the patient and the therapist had not got along well, then the contents of the interview would be negatively toned. In short, the "recovery" or "improvement" index was hardly an objective measure of healthy functioning and can easily be regarded as a reflection of the "health" of the interaction between therapist and patient.

Rosenthal correlated convergence in values with the improvement index and found a remarkably high correlation of .68. To the degree that the patients had shifted their moral values toward the values of their therapists, they reported that the therapy sessions had been positive and beneficial. The therapist's control over the patient's values was thus a central, if not *the* central, element in the patient's later feeling good about the sessions. Although the therapists were not questioned about their patients' progress, we might well presume that their reports would have borne some resemblance to those of the patients. That is, if a therapist can steer the patient's values—in the "correct" direction—the therapy session is subsequently regarded as successful.

A similar pattern of findings was reported by Beutler, Pollack, and Jobe (1978). If patients came to acquire their therapists' attitudes regarding God, communism, social laws, and premarital sexual behavior, they also reported that they felt they had improved. Again, the relation between these two variables (convergence and subjectively rated improvement) was remarkably significant, the correlation being .76.

As pointed out by Beutler (1981), such convergence effects are more pronounced when the therapist's ratings are the criterion for improvement. As a summary statement of this general line of research, it is fair to say that therapists' feelings about the success of the therapy, as well as patients' evaluations of success, are closely intertwined with the extent to which the therapists exert control, in the sense of opinion change, over the patient. We cannot rule out the possibility that "actual" improvement, which would have to be measured independently of patients' and therapists' estimates, might correlate with these opinion change effects. On the other hand, it is difficult to escape the implication that the therapy sessions go especially smoothly when the therapist exerts influence without too much interference or resistance, and that the successful exertion of control over the patient is then built into the overall evaluation of the success of the therapy sessions. The influence can, evidently, take almost any form. For instance, when the patient adopts the therapy language of the therapist and manifests values or attitudes that reflect the therapist's own feelings about the world, the patient is then regarded in a more positive light. It would not be wrong to entertain the possibility that the "correct" manifestation of the self-knower (i.e., showing warmth and empathy or describing one's weaknesses in appropriate clinical language) are acquired by the patient simply through verbal conditioning (Ortlieb, 1973). And we might also imagine that the therapist of the self-knower school may be inclined to reinforce certain classes of behaviors (as demonstrated by Truax, 1966), contrary to the humanistic view that patients should be accepted for "what they are." In short, through rewarding the patient for appropriate interpretations and self-descriptions, the therapist can produce the desired picture of the self-knower. This is our tentative conclusion. However, the clinical-psychology illustration is intended only as an example of a more general point. More broadly, we are interested here in the perception of the self-knower, and particularly in the possibility that having control over a target person will influence one's thoughts about that person's extent of self-knowledge, maturity, or autonomy. An experimental example will show how this process functions.

CONTROL NEEDS WITH RESPECT TO THE SELF-DISCLOSER

Wortman, Adesman, Herman, and Greenberg (1976) worked up an experimental situation in which each respondent became an observer, in this case an "attributor." The respondent was to have contact with a target person (a confederate of the experimenter's) and to make a number of judgments about the person on the basis of the target's self-disclosures. Normally, one would set up such a situation so that different depths of self-disclosure would be evinced, with the expectation that the deeper self-discloser would be perceived as more in tune with the real self.

However, the purpose of this experiment was entirely different. The idea was that the respondent's control over the target person would influence the respondent's judgments about the other's self-knowingness, even if the depth of the self-disclosures was to be held constant. How was control varied? The session was programmed so that the personal disclosures (e.g., "I harbor hostilities against my parents") from the confederate would come relatively late, or early, during the course of the experimental session. In one condition, the confederate "confessed" early, owning up to a list of personal issues early in the session. If we follow the perspective of Wortman *et al.*, then we assume that the respondents in this condition would not sense having control or influence over the disclosures. That is, if the target person (the confederate) blurted them out immediately, the respondents could draw the conclusion that they had not influenced the readiness of the person to disclose, and that the confession would have been made no matter who was there.

In another condition, the confederate waited until later in the interaction to dig into his more intimate personal facets. In this condition, the subjects should have felt that they had something to do with the disclosing; that is, they should have sensed a certain influence or control over the target person.

Following the interaction, the respondents' perceptions of the target person were measured, and Wortman *et al.* explored a number of aspects that bear directly on the self-knower school, that is, personal qualities that are seen as central to the picture of the self-knower. Relative to the confederate who disclosed early in the session (so that the subjects' perceived control should have been minimal), the late-disclosing confederate was regarded as more *secure, mature,* and *genuine,* and there was even a tendency to view that confederate as more open ($p < .08$). All of these results came about simply through the variable of the timing of disclosure; the depth or intimacy of the disclosure was held constant.

A parallel kind of effect can be seen in several other experimental situations. For instance, in a study by Jones and Archer (1976), the confederate (target person) had the apparent option of disclosing to any of several people in the setting. In some cases, the disclosures were addressed only to the subject and not to other individuals, and in other cases, the confederate disclosed to other people as well. In measuring liking for the target person, Jones and Archer found that the subjects liked the confederate more when they had been singled out by the confederate as a "confessor." When the disclosures were scattered around among more people, liking for the confederate dropped correspondingly. In short, if the subject was in a command position and was singled out as the only recipient of the target person's confessions, then the subject showed more liking for the target. It is a short leap to the implication that liking also implies greater attributed self-knowledge. However, the Jones and Archer study does not make this point explicitly, and we shall return to this implication below in the context of two more recent studies.

CONTROL VIA THE TARGET'S SELF-ABASEMENT

It can be documented readily that the observer-subject responds more positively to a target person who is self-abasing (Hoffmann-Graff, 1977): if both favorable and unfavorable self-aspects are communicated, greater liking is apparent when the negative aspects emerge first. Again, a finger points in the direction of control processes. If one's partner begins the conversation by confessing to weaknesses, then the other person (the subject in this case) has the upper hand. If the other person begins with self-aggrandizement, the subject's control or mastery of the situation is threatened. This observation is interesting in light of Mowrer's emphasis (1964) on the therapeutic role of confessing misdeeds and transgressions. Part of the "therapeutic" function could well be giving the therapist or other observer an element of control over the interaction; then in turn, the sense of control would lead the observer to ascribe positive characteristics (e.g., maturity and autonomy) to the patient.

The central point of the foregoing studies is that the subject's (i.e., the observer's) possibility of exerting control over a target person results in a more positive reaction to the target person. In the Wortman et al. study (1976), the positive reaction was very explicitly pertinent to the self-knowledge theme, that is, positivity in the sense of ascribed maturity, genuineness, security, and openness. The other two studies reported above focused more narrowly on the target's attraction, but we might well think that the subject's sense of control over the other would also have affected the imputation of other positive traits (i.e., characteristic "self-knower" traits), had they been measured.

For instance, in a study by Eckert (1987), male and female subjects were requested to describe vividly a conflict situation that they had experienced together with their partner. The 51 subjects were divided at the median according to their appraisal of how positive the conflict situation had been at the outset of the discussion with their partner. The results showed that a favorable resolution of the conflict related positively to ascriptions to the partner of openness ($p < .01$; as in Wortman et al., 1976), individuality ($p < .02$), sociability ($p < .05$), ability to learn more about oneself ($p < .001$) and realistic self-perception ($p < .06$). Although these patterns are correlational, they support the idea (already confirmed in the Wortman et al. experiment) that "self-knowledge" qualities are ascribed to the person in the same manner as other positive qualities. To the extent that the other person is in some important way positive, congenial, or controllable, a more favorable evaluation is to be expected.

The above discussion gives us a start toward a very general hypothesis, one that goes well beyond our opening clinical example and also beyond the experimental literature just summarized. The general hypothesis is best stated in the form of a paradox, as follows: When an observer (or influence agent) can exert control over a second person, there will be a tendency to ascribe positive qualities to that person, a "halo" effect (see Nisbett & Wilson, 1977a; Thorndike, 1920; Wetzel, Wilson, & Kort, 1981). The more predictable the target person, and the more the target can be influenced, the greater will be the observer's (influencer's) tendency to regard the target person in positive terms. The paradox associated with this hypothesis is that these broad, positive evaluations will include dimensions that involve autonomy, independence, or knowing oneself. The implication is that a person who is particularly influenceable, congenial, agreeable, or predictable will be given credit for a good deal of self-knowledge, including the usual accompaniments of self-knowledge, such as autonomy. Simplified, the hypothesis states that people who are objectively controllable and otherwise influenceable will be regarded by the influencer as particularly self-knowing, and as not dependent on others.

THE SELF-KNOWER IN THE EYES OF THE PERCEIVER: TWO INVESTIGATIONS

THE CONGENIAL, AGREEABLE OTHER

The starting point for this research is a simple assumption that a person who is for us (the perceivers) in some respect positive will *therefore* be regarded as positive in other respects. This phenomenon has been called the *halo effect* in personal perception literature (beginning with Thorndike, 1920), and it can be shown to be so strong that even subjects who are informed about its biasing effects show the biasing effect anyway (Wetzel *et al.*, 1981).

Thus, the individual whose attitudes are similar to ours will be given more credit for intelligence or for being less guilty of a crime and will be liked more. The hypothesis can readily be brought into the realm of ascribed self-knowledge in the following manner. If the observer finds another person to be agreeable, congenial, or influenceable and, on a subsequent occasion, is asked to size up that same person on qualities that are associated with self-knowledge, the agreeable other will be given more credit for being self-knowing and autonomous than will a person who is in fact disagreeable or not persuadable. Stated otherwise, a person's judgment about whether another person is self-knowing may be based entirely on the predictability or controllability of that other person. Here is what this hypothesis looks like empirically, in a study by Wicklund and Eckert-Nowack (1989).

The subjects, university students who functioned as observers of a dialogue, were given written materials pertaining to a political discussion. The subjects were told that the topic of the discussion had been a controversial play: *Garbage, City and Death* by Rainer-Werner Fassbinder, a playwright belonging to the liberal political scene. The play had been the subject of considerable controversy before its playing in Frankfurt in the autumn of 1985. The play had been boycotted by the West German Jewish community as well as by several other religious and political groups, on the grounds that Fassbinder had portrayed the main character in his play in an anti-Semitic manner. The issue became a national topic of discussion and generated two major opinion positions: one position was against the showing of the play, and the other opinion charged that the play must be shown on the grounds of the fundamental, constitutionally guaranteed freedom-of-the-arts principle. (The reader is perhaps reminded of similar conflicts in North America, involving conflicts between constitutional principles and extreme ideologies, for example, the right of political extremists to speak and assemble in public places.) Our experiment was conducted at the tail end of this controversy. It was therefore still a salient issue.

Subjects' Opinions

The starting point of the procedure was the measurement of the subject's own opinion regarding the controversy, which was accomplished with three items of the following character:

> What is your position on the protest of the Jewish community in Frankfurt regarding the showing of the Fassbinder play? _____in agreement _____in disagreement

The subject's final opinion (i.e., for the play or against the play) was defined through the dominant trend in answering the three items, so that we could classify each subject as proplay or antiplay.

Procedure

The subject then read three dialogue segments. One of the figures in the dialogue (labeled here the *communicator*) always spoke first and the other figure (labeled the *target person*) spoke second. Our analyses of ascribed self-knowledge and autonomy focused on the target person. In one case, the target person evidenced an opinion that was in full agreement with that of the communicator and continued to show full agreement the entire time (i.e., over the course of all three dialogue segments). This meant, for instance, that the communicator and the target person represented unequivocally a pro-Fassbinder position during the whole dialogue. In other conditions, the same applied, except that the communicator and the target person consistently represented an anti-Fassbinder position. In a parallel set of conditions, the target person consistently *disagreed* with the communicator over the course of the three-part dialogue.

When we regard this scene from the perspective of the observer-subject, we have two conditions that are psychologically interesting. In one case, there was *constant agreement between target person and subject*; in the other case, there was *constant disagreement between target person and subject*. (The other factor, pro- or anti-Fassbinder, was of course present, but it made no difference in the analysis.)

The subject, after having read the set of three dialogues, was asked to rate the target person on a number of dimensions taken directly from the vocabulary of the self-knower school. These were made up of two clusters.

1. *Self-knowledge cluster.* Representative items were "To what extent does the person know himself well?" and "Does the person know his own strengths and weaknesses?" These items were answered on five-point Likert-type scales.

2. *Autonomy cluster.* These items consisted of a series of words that bore on the idea of independence and maturity. They were, for example, *autonomy, critical ability,* and *self-critical.*

The existence of a simple halo effect means that the observer would regard the agreeable or congenial target person as being more positive in almost any respect, including such dimensions as *self-knowledge* and *autonomy*. And this was the case: in both the self-knowledge and autonomy ratings, and also for liking, the target person was seen as more positive in the constant-agreement than in the constant-disagreement condition. This pattern of results held true no matter whether the subjects themselves were pro- or anti-Fassbinder. Thus, the target's particular political-philosophical leaning did not affect the outcome; agreement or disagreement with the observer-subject was the deciding factor. The target person who shared the subject-observer's opinion was regarded by the subject as an autonomous, mature, self-knowing individual.

There was still more to the paradigm. In another set of conditions, the dialogue scenario was arranged so that the target person shifted his opinion during the course of the conversation, always in the direction of the communicator's opinion. This meant that the target person shifted his opinion in the direction of the subject's own opinion for some subjects but, for other subjects, away from the subject's own opinion. Again, the question was: How much self-knowledge and autonomy were ascribed to the target person?, in this case as a function of the direction of the target's opinion change.

The congeniality of the target person for the subject was again the deciding factor. If the target person shifted toward the subject's opinion in the course of the dialogue, the subject rated the target as more self-knowing, autonomous, and likable than the uncongenial target whose opinion moved away from that of the subject.

This result illustrates the paradox hypothesis with which we began the study: A person who is influenceable in a direction that is desirable for the observer is regarded by the observer as a self-knowing, even an autonomous person, relative to a target person who is objectively independent or autonomous. It is also worth noting that these results were found to be independent of the concrete opinion that was represented. In other words, no matter whether the subject represented an antiplay or a proplay opinion on the Fassbinder issue, the agreeable target person was regarded as more self-knowing and autonomous. Thus, contrary to the philosophy embraced by the self-knower school, an accepting, tolerant, open-to-the-world opinion is not automatically taken as an index of self-knowledge. The deciding factor is whether that open and tolerant opinion happens to agree with the opinion of the observer who is making judgments about the target person's self-knowledge.

As the reader has noted, this study did not deal with the subject's own influence attempts; that is, there was no control effort in the sense of the subjects' actually influencing the target person. Rather, control existed in simply knowing that the target person had come around to one's own style of thinking. In the following study, the control theme was carried one step further, to show what happens when the subject's direct influence efforts fail or succeed.

BRINGING ANOTHER PERSON TO SELF-DISCLOSURE

The deeper the self-disclosure, the more the observer is presumed to have reason to conclude that the disclosing person possesses a certain self-knowledge. That may well be, but in the context of the present study, the idea is that the observer's *control* over the disclosures that are emitted is a crucial determinant of the subsequently ascribed self-knowledge. In a context where the observer asks for certain kinds of self-disclosures or for certain topics to be selected, what is the effect when the target person, in the course of disclosing, neglects the exact instructions given by the observer? The following study by Eckert-Nowack (1988) looked at this issue.

All subjects were placed in the role of a "partner" of the experimenter. They were asked to order six questions that were to be responded to by the self-disclosing partner, and in addition, they were to write a new question, also to be used in the self-disclosure sequence. Subsequently, all seven questions were given to the partner, who allegedly went to work on them, writing down self-disclosures to the questions in the order in which they were presented.

Then, the subject received the written self-disclosures from the first six items but was told that the target person was still working on the seventh item (i.e., the item that the subject had written). The critical manipulation came at this point.

Maintenance of Control

The subjects were informed that the answer to the seventh item would be coming shortly, but that they should nonetheless go ahead and fill out a questionnaire that dealt with their impressions of the target person.

Loss of Control

In this condition, the subjects were informed that the target person didn't want the subject to read the answer to the seventh question; the answer was to be read only by the experimenter.

Questionnaire and Results

The subject rated the self-disclosing other on items that should, according to Maslow (1977), represent the self-knowing person. For example, the stimulus person was rated on independence, self-knowledge, self-directedness, autonomy, intelligence, honesty, and other virtues. The outcome of the direct control manipulation was very strong: The person who refused to allow the subject to see the seventh question was regarded as less self-knowing, as less autonomous, and generally—across all items— as less in tune with the self-knower picture spelled out by Maslow.

Given that the subjects in both conditions were given identical information about the target person, one must conclude that the differences had to do directly with the subject's loss of control. Even though the target person in both conditions answered six of the seven questions, the target's nonobedience to the subject in the control-loss condition reduced the subject's estimate of the target's self-knowledge, autonomy, honesty, and so forth. All of this occurred even though the target's refusal would seem—to us at least—to be an objective indication of actual honesty and autonomy. Again, there seems to be some element of truth in our paradoxical hypothesis: The person who is oriented toward control over another gives the other credit for being mature, self-knowing, and autonomous only when the control effort is successful.

AN ORIENTATION TOWARD ASCRIBING TRAITS

We may leave the preceding paradox for a moment and turn to another facet of the observer's ascribing self-knowledge to others. The reader is again referred to the self-knower school's thesis, in which certain indicators, characteristics, or traits are said to signal self-knowledge: autonomy, a sense of humor, warmth, openness, honesty, and the like. For the most part these are trait dispositions (i.e., behavioral potentials) and cannot be observed directly. They are sometimes inferred on the basis of the target person's behavior, and the inference can be mediated by the socially desirable behavior of the target person and by the perceiver's own control motives, among other factors. Now we arrive at a more sweeping question: *What brings the perceiver to infer personality dispositions at all?* As it turns out, the tendency to impute chronic traits to a person can stem from the perceiver's control needs *vis-à-vis* the person who is observed.

One of the first illustrations of the idea comes from an experiment by Miller and Norman (1975). Female subjects were introduced into a game-playing setting involving a series of bargaining maneuvers. Some subjects were made *passive observers*, in that their task was said to involve observing the game playing of two female players. Other subjects, assigned to the *active* condition, found that they would actually be involved in the game with another person. The bargaining game then proceeded and lasted for 30 trials, at which point the subject was asked about her partner (in the active condition) or about one of the players (designated *Player B*) in the passive condition. Looking at the difference between the active and the passive conditions from a control perspective, one can say that the active subjects should have had the strongest control needs with regard to their partners (Player B), and that the passive spectator subject should not have had any major concerns with controlling Player B, who was simply playing against Player A, and not against the subject.

The dependent-variable questions of interest to us were two: "How accurately did Player B's behavior reflect her general personality?" and "How much was it possible to learn about Player B from her behavior?" The game had been arranged so that the behavior of Player B, who actually could not be observed directly, was constant across conditions. Thus, any differences between conditions could be traceable directly to the passive-active distinction. And the results were very informative regarding Miller and Norman's control thesis: when the game took a competitive course, the active subjects were more likely to think that Player B's behavior reflected her personality and were more likely to claim to have learned about Player B from her behavior—all of these tendencies relative to the passive subjects.

In the interest of trying out this phenomenon in our self-knowledge context, let us make a slight leap and assume that we have the therapist or adviser either (1) in the position of a passive observer in an uninvolving dyadic interaction or (2) actively involved in a one-to-one client–therapist interaction. Given the latter, which is surely still more involving than the Miller and Norman paradigm, the desire for control in the setting should lead the therapist or adviser to be oriented toward gaining the maximum possible personality information about the client. What does "gaining personality information" mean? Extrapolating from Miller and Norman's results, it means nothing more than a strong tendency to ascribe fixed personality tendencies to the client or target person. Such intensified ascription may involve the positive side (i.e., "My client definitely has self-insight") or it could, of course, be the contrary, assuming that things do not go the way that the controlling person would like.

Our extrapolation from Norman and Miller can be made still more concrete if we look at the specific adjective ratings occurring after the bargaining session in their study. They found that the active subjects rated Player B as more active, aggressive, and flexible than did the passive subjects. This triad of adjectives reminds us of the Maslow portrait of the self-actualized person: strong, secure, aggressive, and so forth. And interestingly, these observers came to the conclusion that the target person possessed such traits simply through the mechanism of the observer's own control needs, that is, as a result of bargaining with the target person.

Further instances of this phenomenon have been found in a variety of contexts, reported by Berscheid, Graziano, Monson, and Dermer (1976) and by Miller, Norman, and Wright (1978). In the Berscheid *et al.* research, threat to control was varied by giving some of the subjects the expectation that they would later be interacting with the target person, and again, the effect was an increase in the ascription of permanent personality characteristics to the target person. In one of the studies by Miller *et al.* (1978), control was defined empirically in terms of a certain "personal control scale" (Cialdini & Mirels, 1976), and true to expectation, those with the higher control need were more ready to emphasize personality traits in response to the question "Based on the behavior you saw, how well do you think you could describe A's personality to a person who has never met him?"

EXTENDING THE NEED FOR CONTROL: FEELINGS OF INADEQUACY

The desire for control in the paradigms just described was based in the "natural" control desires that people have in routine interactions. But we can push the control concept one step further and propose that people who have a definite insufficiency should have a pronounced desire to gain control in social settings. The effect, still in keeping with the idea of Miller and Norman (1975), should consist of a relationship between inadequate social functioning, or feelings of inferiority, and a propensity to ascribe permanent traits to others.

A study by Funder (1980) is informative in this regard. All of his subjects were given the task of rating stimulus persons, such as a close friend. On each of 20 trait dimensions, the subjects rated the target person by placing a check mark along a six-point continuum between the two poles of the trait (e.g., "subjective—analytical"; "energetic—relaxed"). However, Funder also gave his subjects the option of not using the dimension and, instead, checking "depends on the situation." This system of measurement allows one to see how willing the subjects were to ascribe a personality essence *at all*; they had the freedom to indicate "depends on the situation" for all 20 traits.

Funder then proceeded to differentiate among his subjects in terms of their own personality traits. This personality information was obtained from third parties (i.e., from acquaintances of the subjects), thus ostensibly increasing our faith in the accuracy of these reports. A wide spectrum of personality information (e.g., "copes well under stress"; "feelings of inadequacy") was obtained.

Then, taking the person's own personality as a starting point, Funder looked at the relation between the personality of the subject and the tendency of the subject to rate stimulus persons along the 20 personality dimensions, as opposed to checking the "depends on situation" item. He found that those who used the personality-rating dimensions to a high degree (i.e., those who were ready to make trait inferences) were themselves higher on such dimensions as "feels a lack of personal meaning in life," "thin-skinned," "guileful and deceitful," "does not cope well under stress," "concerned about own inadequacy," "does not respond to humor," "is not calm and relaxed," and "is not cheerful."

The picture portrayed by Funder was that of a socially inadequate individual, generally anxious, who takes things all too seriously. And interestingly, this was exactly the person who was particularly likely to implement the trait dimensions in rating friends and acquaintances. Looking at the results from a control perspective, we can say that this is a person whose control in many social settings is less than assured, and who is inclined, in turn, to view others in terms of personality dimensions, not in terms of others' contexts (i.e., "depends on the situation").

Accordingly, if two individuals—one anxious and sensing lack of control, the other less so—are in a position to ascribe maturity, self-knowledge, and the like to a target person, it is the anxious and uncertain individual who should make the most judgments about the target's self-knowledge. Thus, the observer is not simply an objective trait-information-processing machine. Rather, the observer's momentary need for control, longer term inadequacies, and related states all have a substantial impact on the propensity to use trait terms in analyzing target persons. Once again, it becomes apparent that the observer's evaluation of an individual as a self-knower (i.e., a person who embodies the traits of the self-knower) depends directly on psychological forces acting on the observer.

EXTENDING THE NEED FOR CONTROL AGAIN: INCOMPETENCE IN SPECIFIC REALMS

Suppose that an interviewer, researcher, or therapist is trying to understand the problem of an interviewee or client who is active in a highly complex realm (e.g., an artist, a physicist, or a composer). The interviewer does not have a particularly good idea of how to perform in the realms of art, physics, or composing. In short, the interviewer is seemingly inept in the specific area. This would be a fair description of the usual situation in which a professional, highly trained person is being interviewed, counseled, or treated for psychological problems.

Suppose further that the success of the interview depends on (1) the interviewer's judgments about what the interviewee is lacking (i.e., a kind of diagnosis must be produced) and (2) the interviewer's eventually recognizing when the client has made progress. Given this setting, we put forward the following hypothesis: The more inept the interviewer is in the professional area in which the client is active, the more the interviewer will jump to conclusions about the client's possession of traits, especially traits related to the client's profession. Why should we think this?

Several studies by Koller and Wicklund (1988) and Wicklund and Braun (1987) have begun with a theme much like that just outlined. A respondent is placed in a situation in which there is pressure to comprehend a complex skill; then, the respondent is asked to characterize people who are active in that area. If the respondent lacks experience in the area (e.g., law students or subjects with no experience in painting), or if the respondents are momentarily threatened with regard to their skills, they are then highly prone to use trait language to characterize the activity area.

And conversely, respondents who are themselves competent and active in an area often show an aversion to describing what they do in terms of personality traits (Wicklund & Braun, 1987).

The theoretical bases of these differences are spelled out in the works just cited. For now, let us simply note that threat to competence, or lack of competence, pushes a person in the direction of being dependent on a superficial person-trait or person-descriptor characterization of an area.

Thus, the interviewer, being incapable in the interviewee's area of competence, is very likely—more likely than the interviewee—to be interested in competence-relevant traits. The apparent presence or absence of such traits (self-knowledge markers among others) will in turn be used as the language of the therapy or treatment, and as a result, problems that lie on the level of concrete competence and its execution will not be noticed, at least not by the interviewer.

But let's also try out the other case: the interviewer who also happens to be capable and practiced in the client's area of expertise. In this case, the interviewer should not be so strongly oriented toward the self-knowledge of the client; the interviewer's attention will be more on the task and on the client's concrete background.

The reader can see how such an imbalance of competencies between interviewer and interviewee can lead to considerable confusion regarding the suitability of "self-knowledge." The interviewee will not be terribly concerned about self-knowledge in the broad sense of personality traits (open, warm, flexible, communicative), as the psychological problem is apt to lie in very concrete aspects of the performance execution. But the interviewer, often not having any capacity to appreciate the performance level of an artist, physicist, or other expert, will be much more oriented toward the "self-knowing" self-descriptions of the client.

SUMMARY OF THE FIRST FIVE CHAPTERS

It is our hope that the reader has gained some appreciation of the manifold ways in which self-knowledge has been approached in the existing literature. Here is a brief outline of what we have thus far tried to accomplish:

The kernel of Chapter 1 was an introduction to the issues of "What is the self?" and "How can we gain knowledge of the self?" We arrived at the position that psychology has, for all theoretical and practical purposes, focused its energies on the self as a behavioral potential, and so we have predicated the rest of the book on the idea that this is the self of which people may or may not have knowledge. In addition to the question of "Which self?" the first chapter also dealt with some of the meanings of *knowledge of self*.

Chapter 2 took up the long-standing confusion between two important and separate concepts: the *self* and *knowledge of the self*. We used such examples as Kohlberg's stages of moral development and the James–Lange analysis of emotions in order to communicate the sense of confusion, or running together, of two psychological constructs. Then, based on the theoretical work of Schachter and of Zillmann, we illustrated how previously confused, prematurely mixed constructs can be separated and treated as psychologically separate events.

Chapter 3 introduced the core of the existing view of self-knowledge: the self-knower school. This school of thought equates the presence of a person's self-knowledge with the manifestation of certain criteria, whereby the criteria vary from theorist to theorist and involve such traits as warmth, being free from facades, a sense of humor, flexibility, occupational success, consistency, and a readiness to deprecate oneself. The goal of these self-knowledge conceptions is the pursuit of the self-knower, in that the indices are constructed in order to allow the theorist and others to point to the self-knower—the fully functioning individual, the patient who has been successful in psychotherapy. The third chapter also took a critical attitude toward the self-knower school, charging that the school mixes up the two concepts *self* and *self-knowledge*. The second major issue was the self-knower school's rejection of social influence as a psychologically legitimate source of input into the self and into self-knowledge. The self-knower school is committed to the idea that the important components of one's behavior potential (i.e., self) as well as insight into the self can come about only through direct introspection, devoid of the influence of others and their values.

Chapter 4 continued the critical attitude in an examination of respondents' self-reports. It was charged that the self-knower school allows itself to be wholly dependent on the self-reports as an index of self-knowledge, the problem being that self-reports can have numerous psychological sources, many of them having no bearing whatsoever on the person's internal psychological condition. The self-knower school, in its quickness to eliminate social influence as a contributor to self-knowledge, has also forgotten about social influence factors as explanations of the appearance of "self-knowledge" manifestations. A person's readiness to show socially desirable actions is often enough to account for certain patterns of self-disclosure that lead the observer to ascribe "self-knowingness" to that person.

Chapter 5 switched the focus to the observer: the interviewer, therapist, or researcher. Two aspects of the perception of self-knowledge were brought to light here. One is a paradox, in which the observer can be tricked into ascribing self-knowledge to a person solely on the basis of that person's agreeableness to the observer. The second aspect refers to the relationship between the observer's need for control and the readiness to ascribe personality traits (chronic dispositions) to other people. The chapter indicated that the psychology of the observer is an important contributor to (1) the observer's ascription of self-knowledge and autonomy to a target person and (2) the observer's general tendency to be absorbed with the target person's traits—self-knowledge among others.

THE SYSTEMATIC PERSPECTIVES THAT FOLLOW

The next three chapters take us in the direction of building a systematic theoretical basis for looking at self-knowledge. We shall depart from the preoccupations of the self-knower school, which concentrates on identifying the self-knower, and instead, we will focus on theoretical variables that are responsible for the person's having a sense of behavior potential (i.e., a sense of the self in specific respects), and on variables that are responsible for the coming and going of self-knowledge. However, rather than deal with the person as a self-knowing or non-self-knowing unit, we will analyze self-knowledge in terms of specific knowledge and cognitions, many of which are self-oriented. In this way we hope to convey to the reader a sense of what a systematic, testable, and practical view of self-knowledge looks like.

CHAPTER 6

SELF-KNOWLEDGE

A BASIS IN PERCEPTION, BEHAVIOR, AND LOGIC

In making the jump from the self-knowledge school to the present chapter, we are shifting gears in two important respects. In everything that is reported here, the self and knowledge of the self entail *components* of the person, not the person as a total self-knowing unit. In this sense, we are returning to the line of thinking begun by James (1890), in which single aspects of the human counted as self-aspects that could be criticized or defended individually, and in which there was no thought of dividing human entities into self-knowing and non-self-knowing classes.

By making this shift, we are at the same time preparing ourselves to answer the questions posed at the outset of this book: How do certain components come to be *self*-components, what does it mean to have knowledge of those components, and what are the further implications (for thinking or behavior) of such self-knowledge? Although the theoretical models in this chapter do not offer exhaustive answers, they do enable us to deal with such questions in a researchable manner.

AN ASOCIAL ORIENTATION

Three approaches will be introduced in this chapter: one from McGuire and McGuire (1982), which is a distinctiveness-of-self model; the second from Bem (1965, 1972), called *self-perception theory*; and a third from Fazio and Zanna (1978), on attitude accessibility. None of these is a model of introspection in the sense of the self-knower school. Rather than simply assume that self-knowledge is the product of a seemingly uncaused "looking inward," each of the models discusses particular cue and behavior constellations that lead the person toward knowledge of certain self-aspects. However, there is an overlap with the self-knower approach in that the roots of self-knowledge for McGuire and McGuire, Bem, and Fazio and Zanna are asocial. Nowhere in these formulations do we learn that people owe knowing who they are directly to social influence. Instead, each individual arrives at certain self-perceptions, or an acute awareness of self-aspects, owing to perceptual constellations or to behaviors—one's own behaviors. Society, particularly direct social influence, plays a very minimal role. That is, social influence is (for the present context) not a consideration as an antecedent of self-knowledge.

DISTINCTIVENESS AS THE ONSET OF SELF-KNOWLEDGE

To what extent do individuals come to think spontaneously about certain self-components, such as race, gender, left- or right-handedness, athletic skills, or masculinity or femininity? McGuire and associates (McGuire & McGuire, 1982; McGuire & Padawer-Singer, 1976) have dealt with a setting in which no single facet of a person's self is explicitly mentioned by the interviewer or investigator. They have examined how particular facets of a person become and remain subjectively salient, given that no outside agent directs one's attention to any of those facets.

McGuire and colleagues have implemented variations on a simple device called the "who-are-you" test, confronting people with broad statements such as "Who are you?" or "Tell us about yourself." Subjects then have several minutes to respond, orally or in written form, and of course, one finds a great array of answers in the form of physical characteristics, group memberships, family aspects, attitudes, traits, and the like. Although one can use this technique to find out, for instance, if children list fewer traits than adults (cf. Benenson & Dweck, 1986; Mohr, 1978), the use of this paradigm in the McGuire work has had an entirely different purpose. It has been assumed here that the entire self is not about to be perceived or cognized at any given moment. Rather, the person's acute sense of possessing a self-component (e.g., "smart," "selfish," "Canadian," "Asian") will depend on how distinctive that component is. Although not drawn explicitly from Gestalt psychology, the McGuire idea comes close to the thinking about perception of the 1920s and 1930s, for instance, as formulated by Koffka (1935). If a certain limited aspect of the visual field is black, and the remainder white, attention will gravitate quickly to the "figure," thus, to the minority area (the black area) of the figure. And similarly, if some aspect of oneself is unusual within the immediate environment (e.g., if the person is the only Asian), the person's own attention will gravitate quickly to that characteristic. There will thus be an acute, conscious sense of being Asian, whereas other self-aspects will be neglected (i.e., not focused on).

All of this assumes the prior existence of self-components, and presumably, all of those self-components will have their impact on behavior even if the person does not focus on them directly. This will become an issue later. But behavior aside, the central element of this model is the perceptual feature: The distinctiveness of an element results in the person's tuning in on it cognitively, and for the present, we will treat this kind of self-focusing as an instance of self-knowledge. And now, what does the McGuire approach look like more concretely?

McGuire and McGuire (1981) used the "tell-us-about-yourself" approach with a sample of 1,000 schoolchildren, ranging from the 5th to the 12th grade. One of the self-dimensions of interest to the authors was height. We need to begin by asking what *distinctiveness* means with respect to height, and here, the authors answered the question straightforwardly. "Average" height was operationalized as being within one inch of the average height for one's age level and gender; "distinct" (i.e., very tall or very short) meant being five inches above or below the average for one's gender and age group. This typifies the McGuire approach: First, establish whether the person is relatively distinct on a given self-related dimension, and then examine responses to the "tell-us-about-yourself" item to find out what self-dimensions are mentioned spontaneously by the respondents. Here is what happened:

Among the respondents who were of average height (for their respective gender and age groups), only 17% mentioned height as part of their self-descriptions, in contrast to 27% among the children who were distinct (very tall or very short) with respect to height. Similar results have been obtained with other dimensions, including left-handedness versus right-handedness, race, weight, and gender.

The results do not prove that a certain self-aspect is forever dominant for a person. Rather, McGuire and McGuire showed that the person's distinctiveness against the backdrop of that person's surroundings is the critical factor. For instance, just because being black is distinctive across a whole city or nation does not mean that black must be distinctive in every social setting. And to be sure, as the proportion of minority respondents within a given setting increases, distinctiveness drops, and so does the tendency to mention one's ethnic group in response to the "who-am-I" question (McGuire, McGuire, Child, & Fujioka, 1978).

Theoretically, one could extend the McGuire paradigm to any realm of the self mentioned by James (1890)—beyond the material and social, and into the self-aspects that we have dealt with thus far, that is, behavioral potentials. The principle remains the same. If an aspect of oneself stands out as unique against the surroundings of a homogeneous setting, that self-aspect will automatically come to the fore in one's perceptions; it will also be mentioned more often.

RELEVANCE TO SUBSEQUENT BEHAVIOR

The distinctiveness formulation offers us a bold start on a systematic view of self-knowledge, even if it is a minimal start. McGuire and McGuire (1982) pointed the way toward a systematic variable—distinctiveness within the context of the surroundings—as an onset of thinking about oneself. In referring to the perceptual dominance or salience that is set in motion by distinctiveness, the authors implicitly imbedded their work in an old tradition of Gestalt psychology (Koffka, 1935), as well as in similar formulations that have pointed to the relation between distinctiveness and a tendency to locate causality in distinct events and persons (see Duval, 1976; McArthur & Post, 1977). But in one respect, the analysis falls short. McGuire and McGuire wrote very little about the consequences of self-aspect salience. People may well be acutely aware of their extreme weight or extreme athletic prowess, but it remains unclear whether this awareness has any further implications for behavior or thinking. That is, the existence of the self-aspect (e.g., extreme weight or athletic potential) may well have its impact on further behavior even if the aspect is *not* subjectively salient. This is an issue that will surface again later in this chapter as well as in subsequent chapters.

ONE'S OWN BEHAVIOR AS THE SOURCE OF SELF-KNOWLEDGE

BEGINNING WITH RADICAL BEHAVIORISM

Bem (1972) was the most explicit of all the authors we cite in rejecting the possibility of the human's having direct, natural contact with inner psychological states. In looking at statements such as "I am depressed," "I am biased in favor of older people," and "I know myself well," Bem charged that none of these is based on direct perceptual contact with an inner "object" of perception. Bem followed Skinner (1957) in assuming that the terms a person uses to describe private events (pain, emotion, attitudes, and impulses) are learned in social exchanges.

For example, when a child falls and cries, the parents are likely to supply the child with a verbal repertoire ("It hurts, it burns, it stings"), which the child then comes to use when similar kinds of injuries arise. It is similar with emotions, as our previous discussion of Schachter (1964) and Zillmann (1978) indicated, and also with attitudes, motives, conflicts, and the like. According to the Skinnerian (and Bemian) position, children come to describe their internal states in the same language that parents and others use to describe the child's internal states. The parents, of course, do not have direct access to the inner, subjective event; their descriptions are based on the immediate context plus what the child does. Bem's position is that the child has no greater direct, subjective access to those internal events and so uses the language supplied by parents and others.

SELF-KNOWLEDGE AS PURE LOGICAL INFERENCE

The human being with whom Bem began is thus a person who has a certain verbal repertoire. Such phrases as "negative attitude toward X,Y,Z," "fright," "ache in lower abdomen," "hostility," and "need for social contact" have all been learned. All of these refer to internal states of one's own organism; on the other hand, it is Bem's thesis that a person has little, if any, direct access to inner events. How is it, then, that such terms are used at all? How can a human use words that refer to self-knowledge when there is no direct contact with internal events? Bem's (1972) answer is this:

> Individuals come to "know" their own attitudes, emotions, and other internal states partially by inferring them from observations of their own overt behavior and/or the circumstances in which this behavior occurs. (p. 5)

A second assumption by Bem renders the first one even more obvious: Individuals are frequently much like external observers, having no greater direct access to their own internal conditions than observers. Both observers and self-observers depend on the behaviors and the context and, using these in combination, come to an inference about the self. Therefore, self-knowledge is thought by Bem to be equivalent to an inference, a kind of logical guess, pieced together on the basis of behavior and context, rather than being the result of direct self-observation.

This thesis has often been extended to a liking for certain objects. If a person is paid to undertake an activity, the payment serves as a plausible reason for performing the activity. When asked for liking for the activity, or if the energy and time subsequently devoted to the activity are mea-sured, it can be found that lower (or no) payment is associated with greater time expenditure (Lepper, Greene, & Nisbett, 1973). In the language of self-perception theory, the presence of an external cause for performing an activity reduces the person's certainty that something "inside" is motivat-ing the activity. This seemingly logical inference, which both the observer and the self-observer are capable of making, constitutes a bit of self-knowledge—but a self-knowledge that is pieced together on the basis of one's behavior and one's circumstances.

Most of the extensions of Bem's reasoning involve something quite parallel to the Lepper *et al.* (1973) experiment. The subject decides to undertake an activity, and this decision serves as the starting point for the self-analysis. If the behavior is undertaken freely, the subjects (as well as noninvolved observers) appear to infer that they are motivated, that is, that they like the activity, and that they are attracted to the goals involved. If the activity is forced (e.g., rewarded) from the outside, the effect is a reduced tendency to impute high motivation for the activity or high liking of the goal object. Such an inference seems entirely logical, and perhaps the most interesting aspect of Bem's research is that the analysis does indeed seem to work, no matter whether people are analyzing their own behavior or other people are analyzing that behavior. Both the observer and the self-observer consider the type of behavior enacted, plus the strength of the behavior-eliciting circumstances, and then make a judgment about the person's degree of motivation or attitude.

IS THE INFERRED BEHAVIORAL POTENTIAL A VACUUM?

Obviously, a committed disciple of the self-knowledge school would not be happy with the behavioristic self-knowledge formulation of Bem. All of Bem's examples, all of the experimental illustrations and proofs, and all of the implications point to self-knowledge as nothing more than an inference composed of the person's behavioral direction and the amount of environmental pressure to behave in a certain way. The inference, worded in the language of attitudes, emotions, or even traits, involves applying a name to a vacuum, to an internal state that is, in fact (according to Bem), not directly sensed or perceived. Is this a perversion of the sense of self-knowledge?

That would depend on the reader's perspective. Clearly, Bem and co-workers have been able to show that humans are not entirely in direct touch with their internal processes; otherwise, the respondents' self-di-rected statements would not be so easily influenceable by information about the behavior context. Thus, at a minimum, the self-perception approach has shown how flexible—and perhaps also how uncertain—the human is in arriving at judgments regarding internal psychological states. And still more important for our present purposes is the scientific character of self-perception theory. Bem at least stipulated conditions under which a strong or weak inference will be drawn about an internal state or a psychological condition. It is up to the critic to prove that the human does have valid and direct perceptual access to internal events, independent of the logical inference processes that clearly go on.

SELF-PERCEPTION THEORY AND PERSONALITY DISPOSITIONS

All of the experimental illustrations of the self-perception thesis have involved transitory states of the person, such as emotions (e.g., fear; see Bandler, Madaras, & Bem, 1968) or attitudes (Bem, 1965). All of these paradigms have entailed the subjects' reaction to external objects (e.g., a shock-generating device or a social object toward which an attitude is directed). In such paradigms, the subject shows a positive or negative leaning—an attraction or withdrawal—with regard to a concrete object or person, and the ascription of self-knowledge that follows is of the nature of "I am afraid of the machine" or "I like a certain police force." In referring to these kinds of inferences as "self-knowledge," Bem (1972) limited knowledge about oneself to attitudes, and thus to attractions (or aversions) to concrete, external objects. Therefore, the self-knowledge inference does not seem to penetrate very deeply into the person, because the inference is barely more than a description of behavior—a behavioral tendency toward specific objects.

On the other hand, Bem (1972) pointed toward the possibility that personality dispositions may also have their roots in self-perception. And in the case of personality dispositions, we are not dealing strictly with an orientation toward an object; rather, the disposition refers to a chronic tendency of the person, across time, objects, and situations. The following illustrates this line of thought.

Bem referred to a setting in which subjects were asked to perform a small favor for an interviewer, for instance, to place a small sign in a window of their homes supporting safe driving (Freedman & Fraser, 1966). After a two-week interval, the same subjects were again contacted, and this time a much larger request was made. Interestingly, having complied with the first (minor) request greatly enhanced the chances of the subjects' complying with the second request, even if the second request had little in common with the first one. In discussing their findings, Freedman and Fraser suggested that the subjects came to assume, after having assented to the first request, that they were "the sort of persons who do favors for others." In other words, one could characterize this change as the forming or changing of a personality disposition.

The Locksley and Lenauer Elaboration

On the other hand, Bem did not devote much discussion to the above issue, nor to the question of how a behavior directed toward a concrete object or person leads one to infer a broad personality disposition such as extraversion or warmth. This leap was made in grand style by Locksley and Lenauer (1981), whose basic reasoning is Bem's self-perception theory. Their analysis proceeds as follows:

The starting point (just as for self-perception theory) is the person's asking "Who am I?" in some specific respect. In Bem's example, the question usually takes the form of an attitude ("Do I like police?"); in the Locksley and Lenauer extension, the question is more "To what degree am I aggressive or passive?" The second step is the examining of pertinent behavioral scenarios from one's past—episodes that bear directly on the passive-versus-aggressive issue. After looking at the sum of these cases (or presumably a sample of them), the person is said to come to a conclusion in the form of a subjective probability statement. For instance, if the person finds about 75% aggressive and 25% passive in the critical, relevant cases, then the conclusion is approximately, "I feel subjectively that I am quite (but not totally) aggressive."

The Locksley and Lenauer notion sounds as if it would be the ideal answer to a behavior-based self-knowledge. Instead of basing one's knowledge just on a recent instance of behavior, as in Bem's analysis, the person goes on a historical search through relevant behavioral episodes and then flushes self-knowledge directly out of the dominant behavioral stream. Unfortunately, we have to leave this theme on a pessimistic note: Locksley and Lenauer provided neither concrete examples nor research evidence of how this process functions, and to our knowledge, there is no demonstration that such a process takes place in the form described. If there is a self-knowledge that is derived (i.e., inferred) from the behavioral level, then it would seem to be limited to knowledge of what one has done to concrete objects or other persons. Self-knowledge takes the form of "I like swimming" (because I do it a lot) or "I am afraid of spiders" (because I always run from them).

WHERE SELF-PERCEPTION THEORY STOPS SHORT

In contrast to the self-knower school, we have concluded that a prerequisite for a scientific treatment of self-knowledge is the separation of the human, as a unit, from individual components of the self. Self-perception theory accomplishes this separation very adequately, in that discrete behaviors form the basis of inferences about self-components (i.e., in this case, attitudes). Second, we had hoped that the ideal self-knowledge theory would be able to stipulate how self-knowledge goes into gear. What does it mean to have knowledge of a self-aspect, and how can the human be prompted or educated to know that aspect? In this respect, self-perception theory is seriously flawed: The analysis of the self, according to Bem, begins with the person's being confronted by others with the questions "Who are you?" or "What do you think about _____?" Thus prompting from the outside (i.e., cues to think about one's attitudes or other aspects) is the starting point. Unfortunately, the necessity of such external promptings means that self-perception theory offers no systematic variables that instigate self-knowledge.

The issue is handled no more completely in the Locksley and Lenauer approach. They began their process with the person who happens to ask, for example, "How neurotic am I?" But why does the person happen to ask this question? The Bemian solution (forcing the self-knowledge inquiry through a questionnaire) is obviously no answer. Thus, one would still like to know how it is that people come to be curious about their own behavioral potential.

Self as Separate from Self-Knowledge

Are the self and knowledge of the self two separate psychological events? Self-perception theory is not in a position to recognize the differentiation, for a very simple reason. The idea central to Bem's thinking (1965) is drawn from Skinnerian philosophy, which is skeptical about the presence or measurability of internal psychological states. Bem's beginning position, for which the theory has been widely acclaimed, is that attitudes are either nonexistent as an enduring entity or else so weak that they are easily supplanted by subsequent inferences based on recent behaviors (an illustration is offered in an experiment by Bem & McConnell, 1970).

Thus, if attitudes (and other internal events) do not have an independent existence within the behaviorist framework, one can scarcely speak of an enduring self. And self-knowledge? Obviously, self-knowledge, in whatever form, cannot be enduring either. It all comes once the person is prompted to produce an attitude, a value, or an emotion. Suddenly, the person stops to examine a recent relevant behavior ("I ran from the spider"), plus situational exigencies, and makes the logical inference ("I have a fear of spiders"). This statement is, then, self-knowledge *as well as self.*

This is because the Bemian self goes no deeper, nor is it more permanent, than the verbal inference.

Consequences of Self-Knowledge

The other question we raised earlier was whether knowledge of the self makes a difference in further thinking or in further behaving, or even in changes in the self. On this point, self-perception theory is silent, as it is strictly a theory about logical inferences, not about the motivations to behave that stem out of those inferences. At most, self-perception theory would allow a highly cautious statement. If the person has not recently behaved in the relevant area (e.g., with respect to a certain racial group), then there is certainly no attitude present. Accordingly, the direction taken in behavior will be given 100% by other kinds of factors, such as (1) existing habits toward the reference group; (2) interpersonal influence; (3) goal orientation; or (4) perhaps other factors that were named earlier by Wicker (1969).

If the reader has been disappointed with self-perception theory as an answer to the self-knowledge issue, then the third development in this chapter, to follow, should be welcomed. In their theoretical model, Fazio and Zanna (1978) paid considerable attention to both (1) the separation of the self from knowledge of the self and (2) the conditions instigating knowledge of the self. Let us see what this model looks like.

ATTITUDE ACCESSIBILITY

An attitude may be regarded as a facet of the self, as a bit of behavioral potential that is limited to potential actions directed toward a given class of objects. Thus, attitudes are directed toward consumer items, racial groups, clothing styles, and particularly political parties. The approach summarized here (Fazio, 1986; Fazio & Zanna, 1978; Zanna & Fazio, 1982) begins with the assumption that an attitude is indeed a latent disposition to behave positively or negatively toward some event or object. Unlike in the Bem framework, attitudes are treated as a durable aspect of the person; they are by no means equivalent to instances of behavior. On the other hand, as pointed out by Fazio (1986), the attitude is not always cognitively activated, or in simpler terms, people do not always think about every attitude in their repertoire. As a result, many other factors are likely to override attitudes in influencing behavior, such as the norms of the behavior setting (e.g., whether being liberal or conservative is polite). The role of such competing factors was examined rather exhaustively by Wicker (1969) and was taken up again by Bagozzi, Yi, and Baumgartner (1990).

The attitude must be "accessed from memory" if it is going to influence behavior. In the words of Fazio (1986):

> If I hold a positive attitude toward a given object and if my attitude has been activated, then I am likely to notice, attend to, and process primarily the positive qualities of the object. (p. 212)

And in turn, persons whose attitudes are momentarily activated—that is, persons who have a momentary "self-knowledge" of the attitude—are apt to define the attitude object and the relevant surroundings in terms of the attitude, with the result that their actions will coincide with the attitude. This is the kind of consistency that is regarded historically as the hallmark of the self-knower.

But how does the attitude become transformed from a latent entity (i.e., something about which one does not think) into a central, focused-on part of the self? One of the dominant answers in the Fazio and Zanna literature is *behavior*. The person who has recently behaved toward the attitude object is likely to think about that behavioral leaning or, in other words, about that attitude. Empirically, generating this variety of self-knowledge takes the following form.

Attitudes toward Intellectual Tasks

The first step of an experiment by Regan and Fazio (1977) involved making sure that all of the subjects had developed attitudes, in this case attitudes toward five intellectual-type puzzles. In a relatively passive condition, called the "indirect experience" condition, the respondents were shown previously worked examples of each puzzle and also listened to the experimenter relating the routes to the solutions. The subjects were easily able to state their attitudes toward each of the puzzles afterward. In the "direct experience" condition, they were first allowed to play with the puzzles and thereby to gain direct behavioral experience. After this initial phase, the subjects' attitudes were measured.

Second, all subjects were introduced into a "free-play" behavioral situation, in which they could play with any of the puzzles they wished to. Regan and Fazio then measured the degree of consistency between behavior and the attitudes that had been assessed just before the free-play period. There was a stronger consistency between attitude and free-play behavior among the subjects who had initially had behavioral experience with the attitude objects, that is, the puzzles.

A variety of further studies (see Fazio, 1986) suggest that making the behavior salient does in fact bring the respondents' attitudes to the forefront of their thinking. If the behaviors pertinent to the attitude are first enacted, subjects then respond to the attitude measure more quickly in a reaction-time framework than when the behaviors are not so immediate.

SELF-KNOWLEDGE VIA THE REPEATED EXPRESSION OF THE ATTITUDE

What exactly is the antecedent of self-knowledge within the attitude accessibility model? Although the focus is on overt, attitude-relevant behavior, the model allows *any* event that heightens the cognitive accessibility of the attitude to be appropriate. For instance, Powell and Fazio (1984) varied nothing more than the number of times that subjects were asked to indicate their attitudes; the speed with which the subjects could then express their attitudes was strongly affected. Prior expression appears to heighten the immediacy, availability, or salience of the attitude. If we look at the kind of interpretation given to these effects, it appears quite straightforward:

> Each time one is asked to make any evaluative judgment of an attitude object, the strength of the association between the object and its overall goodness or badness is enhanced. As a result, the attitude is more accessible from memory. (Powell & Fazio, 1984, p. 145)

Although the subjects' subsequent consistency between attitude and behavior was not measured, it stands to reason that repeated expressions of attitude would also increase consistency, given that the two kinds of phenomena—behavioral consistency and quickness of attitude expression—hang together when we look at this research tradition as an entirety.

A STEP BEYOND SELF-KNOWLEDGE AS ROOTED IN BEHAVIOR

We might step back a bit from the internal workings of the Fazio and Zanna process and ask how their findings contribute to an understanding of self-knowledge. First of all, their notion overcomes the difficulty of treating the person as a self-knowing unit and of trying to identify that unit in terms of traits (e.g., warmth and consistency). The self is regarded here as a set of attitudes; there are no constraints on the type of attitude that can come into the person's cognitive view. Thus, Fazio and Zanna began with the person who holds a view of something: that attitude may be highly conservative, liberal, tolerant, or intolerant; it may be a view that is addressed to mundane, everyday happenings and objects, or to significant social issues. The important point is that the investigator has reason to think that the person has an attitude, however latent or weak that attitude may be.

Second, Fazio and Zanna allowed that attitudes are not always thought about, even when they happen to be immediately relevant to future actions. An individual who is in conflict about which of several puzzles to play with (see Regan & Fazio, 1977), or about which political party to join does not necessarily act on the basis of a conscious or cognitively available attitude. Instead, the person's behaviors can simply "go into gear," sometimes on the basis of automated responses (see Fazio, 1986), sometimes on the basis of social pressures. Translating the Fazio and Zanna language into our context, we can say that people who hold attitudes seldom have self-knowledge of those attitudes, even when attitude-based action is necessary.

What, then, instigates self-knowledge? There is no premise here that people seek out self-knowledge in the sense of attempting to become more cognitively attuned to their true attitudes. Rather, certain circumstances force the person to be acutely attuned to a given attitude, and this cognitive attunement is then regarded as self-knowledge. Note that such self-knowledge is in no way knowledge of one's whole being, nor does it mean that the person is forever more a self-knower. It means only that the individual, at a given moment, is particularly aware of a given attitude.

In their discussions, Fazio and Zanna pointed repeatedly to *behavior* as a route to such self-knowledge. A good method of increasing this focusing on attitude is to allow the person to behave in some way pertinent to the attitude just before stating the attitude. To the degree that the behavior is close in time (i.e., occurs just before the statement of one's attitude), the speed with which the attitude is expressed and also the consistency between that attitude and subsequent behaviors are enhanced.

Unlike in the self-perception analysis of Bem (1972), Fazio and Zanna took their analysis in the direction of "What is the attitude good for?" or, in terms of our current question, "Does self-knowledge have any implications for further thinking or behavior?" The answer should be evident from our discussion: A cognitive attunement to one's attitude, as self-knowledge, has very direct ramifications for the person's subsequent behaving.

WHERE THE ANALYSIS STOPS

How broad is self-knowledge within this attitude-accessibility model? Just as with all of the empirical work surrounding self-perception theory, the idea is limited explicitly to attitudes. Rather than dealing with self-knowledge as a knowledge of any aspect of one's behavioral potential, we are asked here to focus especially on behavioral potential with respect to given objects and, even more concretely, on the person's potential to experience negative or positive affect with regard to those objects. Much as in self-perception theory, the self-knowledge in this case is limited to

statements such as "I dislike snakes" or "I am in favor of the Democrats."
On the other hand, the range of attitudes to which the model has been
applied is impressive. Among others, Fazio, Zanna, and their colleagues
have studied the issues of legalized abortion, the Equal Rights Amend-
ment, the plea of not guilty by reason of insanity, gun control, mandatory
retirement age, nuclear power plants (Powell & Fazio, 1984), the housing
crisis on a campus (Regan & Fazio, 1977), participation in psychological
research (Fazio & Zanna, 1978), religious customs (Fazio, Herr, & Olney,
1984), and a host of others. Although broader dispositions such as ethno-
centrism, sex guilt, or punitiveness have not been studied within the
paradigm, there is no evident reason why such an extension is not possible.
As long as the trait-relevant behaviors are enacted just before the person's
making the self-report, the same kinds of effects should be found as for
attitudes.

SELF-KNOWLEDGE WITHOUT SOCIAL INFLUENCE

One of our criticisms of the self-knower school in Chapter 3 was
directed at the school's *asocial* conception of the self-knowing human. The
general thrust of the various members of the self-knower school is that
social influence can only interfere with the person's accurate sense of the
true self-kernel, and that all aspects that are taken over from society are
facadelike. The assumption is that deep and accurate self-knowledge is to
be won only by introspection, by shunting aside the influences and socialization efforts of others.

Self-perception theory and also the notions of Fazio and Zanna are
equally asocial, but they have come to terms with a problem that plagues
the self-knower school. The problem with the self-knower school is that the
process by which a given instance of behavioral potential is to be known
is never stipulated. Instead of beginning with a given behavioral tendency
(or potential), such as an attitude or a value, the self-knower school
proceeds to regard the human as an indivisible unit and then tries to
recognize the hero by looking for certain indices of self-knowledge. The
models discussed in this chapter make no pretense of addressing a "self-
knowing human, having insight into the 'real' self." They are considerably
more modest and begin by analyzing just one part of the self at a time,
limiting the whole undertaking to attitudes, and thus to tendencies directed toward concrete objects. The underlying idea focuses on overt behaviors. Within self-perception theory, self-knowledge comes about
through the combination of two events: The person is confronted with the
necessity of answering "What is your attitude about _____?" And the
person has behaved in some relevant way. On the basis of these two

events, the person draws a logical inference and makes an attitude statement ("I am fond of _____ ").

The Fazio and Zanna approach is equally asocial, again drawing on behavior as fundamental to self-knowledge. And from their perspective, behaving in an attitude-relevant manner is sufficient to bring conscious attention to the already existing attitude. Or in other words, self-knowledge with respect to the attitude comes into play through the person's behaving.

Equally asocial is the McGuire and McGuire alternative to self-knowledge. But in their case, prior behavior is not the key; a simple perceptual principle is the prerequisite to the self-knowledge process. One's attention is drawn to characteristics that are unusual relative to the immediately surrounding environment. In fact, a very similar postulate is explicit in Shibutani (1961), a sociologist.

Each of these models departs from the self-knower school in that the self is not treated as an indivisible mass. One self-facet at a time is examined, and either one's behavior or the oddity or distinctiveness of a personal trait causes the psychological onset of self-knowledge. None of these three approaches deals with society's building a self into the individual; none of the three treats social influence or social contact as the prerequisite of self-knowledge. This is the task of the next chapter, which represents the human as an entirely socially based entity, derived solely from subtle and direct social influence.

SELF-KNOWLEDGE

THE VERBAL CONTENT DIRECTLY FROM THE SOCIAL CONTEXT

SELF-KNOWLEDGE AS ATTACHING LABELS TO ONE'S OWN PERSON

The initial focus of this chapter is on the influence of one's group or society on applying labels to oneself, such as "I am sociable" or "I am a capable conversationalist." Our present context treats such self-descriptions as elements of knowledge that stem from outside. Not postulating a core internal self or a kernel of one's essence to be discovered, this chapter points the way toward a causal analysis of how people know themselves, taking a straightforward perspective. Self-knowledge is treated as coming to know how to characterize oneself in terms of trait or disposition labels. The behaviorist element of the previous chapter is not present here; the present perspective assumes that self-characterizations originate in social contexts, not in a person's own behaviors.

A chief problem of the self-knowledge school is its total reliance on self-descriptions, and in looking at the issue more carefully, we noted that self-descriptions can come about totally through factors such as trying to create a desirable impression. This chapter can thus be viewed as a systematic treatment of such self-descriptions and consists largely of the question: When and how do people come to apply behavioral-potential terms to themselves?

The self-knower school skirts the issue of what self-knowledge means among people who do not have the appropriate vocabulary at their fingertips. However, there is a psychology of this cultural and developmental issue, and the important idea is that self-knowledge, as expressed in trait descriptions, does not stem from a vacuum, nor directly from one's "true self." Rather, one has to look to the social milieu, even if this would amount to heresy within the self-knower school.

Dennis Bromley

Contrasting sharply with a self-knower-school interpretation of self-references, Bromley (1977) laid the emphasis on the functional value of trait terms within one's culture. His procedure entails asking respondents to describe themselves and others (such as a liked or disliked other), and the characteristic result is along the lines of depictions of the person's age, national origin, and type of employment; various trait terms such as *cheerful* and *stodgy*; and characterizations of the person's external appearance. Bromley sorted the results of such surveys into numerous categories, including traits, abilities, self-concept, and social position. But more important than the characterization of these self- and other-descriptions is his simple notion that the implementing of such personality terms is functional in allowing people to draw comparisons and contrasts between people. Needless to say, something that is functional for the society may well be regarded as learned from the society. The issue of the acquisition of these person descriptions is taken up in the following section.

WHEN DO CHILDREN BEGIN TO IMPLEMENT PERSONAL DESCRIPTIONS?

Benenson and Dweck (1986) looked at a sample of children ranging in age from 5 to 11. The children were given vignettes from their everyday school life, portraying successes and failures in both social and academic realms. The children were asked to provide explanations for these various events. For instance, as an example of others' failure in the social realm, they were requested to think of classmates who "have a lot of kids who don't like to play with them." The question the subject was to answer was simply "Why do they have a lot of kids who don't like to play with them?"

The children's accounts were coded into categories, and for our purposes, the interesting category was trait explanations. Fewer than 10% of the kindergarten children used trait explanations, whereas about 60% of the 10-year-old respondents offered traitlike accounts of the circumstances.

There are two possible perspectives on findings such as these. First, it is conceivable (with a stretch of the imagination) that the youngest children do not, in fact, have stable sets of potentials (i.e., personality dispositions) in the social and academic realms. Their development is constantly in flux, being redefined, and it follows naturally that these children would not be inclined to use terms that refer to a stable human being in order to characterize either their own failures or successes or those of age-mates. The second possibility, which in a moment will be made still more plausible, is that the use of such terms is little more than a reflection of verbal learning, of the acquisition of a trait-term repertoire during the course of socialization. Why would we think that the second possibility is more plausible?

Miller (1984) demonstrated similar age differences in the use of personality terms, but in addition, she noted strong differences between two cultures, based on samples in India and Chicago. The Chicagoans (let us say Americans) were much more generous in the use of personality language to explain everyday human incidents (e.g., a traffic accident) than were the Indians, whereas the Indians were relatively more apt to characterize the event in terms of the situational context. It seems rather unlikely that Americans possess more personality dispositions than do Indians, or more behavior potential, and we are therefore led to think that the use of personality language does not depend on the nature or breadth of one's own behavioral repertoire. The implication about the children in the Benenson and Dweck study should be clear: It begins to look as if the younger children did not use personality language simply because they had not yet learned to use it, and that the magic age of 10 or so reflects a cumulation in linguistic training.

Were the self-knower school to compare the self-knowledge of children and adults, or the self-knowledge of Indians and Americans, it would be easy to come to the conclusion that children and people in India, or perhaps particularly Indian children, have little self-knowledge. The conclusion would, of course, be based on the results of linguistic training, not on the individuals' actual dispositions or potentials. As we saw in Chapter 3, Jourard (1961) came to a similar, presumably ethnocentric conclusion in suggesting that Americans are "healthier" than either English or Germans. His conclusion stemmed from the different self-disclosure rates of English and American subjects. What he had overlooked is that a firm grounding in personality language is no doubt conducive to making deep-sounding self-disclosures. Had Jourard compared children and adults, he would have had to conclude that the adults were healthier (i.e., better self-disclosers) than the children, at least in the realm of disclosing traits.

"What Will Change about You?"

The developmental sequences just described are by no means limited to abstract explanations of hypothetical behavioral instances. Even more on target for our self-knowledge theme is a study by Mohr (1978), whose respondents consisted of first-graders, third-graders, and sixth-graders. These subjects were asked an assortment of personal questions designed to elicit self-related remarks, such as "What will change about you when you grow up?" Obviously, this was an opportunity for the respondent to show deep self-knowledge, probing into motives, wishes, problems, and all of what we might want to call "classical" self-insight.

The children's responses were categorized three ways:

1. In the *external* category was the naming of physical or blatant demographic characteristics, such as name, age, or possessions. This category is approximately what William James intended by his "material self."

2. *Behavioral* was the second category. This is, of course, the measure appropriate to the behavioristic analyses by Bem or Locksley and Lenauer; categorized here were simple references to one's own behavior.

3. The *internal* category contained statements referring to feelings, thoughts, and other states that were rated as internal.

The differences among age groups with reference to the item "What will change about you . . . ?" were striking. The first-graders depended almost totally on the *external* category for their self-descriptions; the third-graders evidenced a slight shift away from the category, making more use of *behavior*; and the sixth-graders left the external qualities behind in favor of *internal* self-descriptors. We do not need to emphasize the point that the apparent self-knower (i.e., the sixth-graders in this study) were the product of linguistic civilizing. Certainly, a self-description of "I will be more thoughtful, modest, and spiritual" (the sixth-graders) sounds more like self-knowledge to many psychologists than does "I will become tall and earn much money" (the first-graders). The simple point here is that the first-graders did not have the verbal repertoire with which to make such profound-sounding self-observations.

KNOWLEDGE OF THE SELF AS AN INDIRECT EFFECT OF SOCIAL INTERACTION

Up to this point, we have continued to treat self-knowledge strictly in terms of labeling. Whether there is any actual behavioral potential underlying the labels has been left aside as an open question; our concentration has been on the question of the use of self-directed labels. But at this juncture, with the introduction of symbolic interactionism, we begin to get a hint of the relation between the socially determined labeling of oneself and one's actual behavior potentials.

THE LOOKING-GLASS SELF

A good starting point is Cooley (1902). His idea was that we know who we are by means of what we think others think of us. Starting without any self-concept at all, people gradually build up a sense of where they stand on different dimensions simply through thinking about how others define or construe them. Cooley's idea is so often repeated—frequently in contextless form—that we seldom gain an appreciation of its importance. In effect, Cooley was describing a subtle social-influence process. Our self-concepts are constructed not simply through the *direct* influence of others ("You're a jerk"), although that can of course take place, but through taking others' perspectives toward ourselves. A characteristic example is a person's thoughts following an interaction. One person has just talked with a powerful other. The other has discussed a variety of issues, and after the conversation, the person asks himself, "What did she mean by that? It seems that she was impressed by my honesty." And in this manner, according to Cooley (1902), we internalize the opinions of those around us, drawing them into our repertoire of self-descriptions.

Direct tests of the idea are surprisingly rare, but we will sketch one stemming from Fazio, Effrein, and Falender (1981), in which the paradigm offered subjects a chance to internalize certain personality traits. The subject was asked to respond to a set of questions, some of which were tailored to introverted people (e.g., "What things do you dislike about loud parties?"), the assumption being that the experimenter's expectations about the subject's personality would be implied by such questions. The subject read and then answered eight such questions, all implicitly predicated on the subject's introversion. In theory, the expectations built into such a communication setting should have convinced the subject that the immediate social environment expected a generally introverted orientation. All of the questions were leading ones, assuming between the lines that the subject had introverted leanings.

Subsequently, the subjects' extent of introversion or extraversion was measured in two different ways meant to reveal whether the subjects had, through this subtle paradigm, convinced themselves that they were indeed introverted. The first measure was the usual questionnaire type, assessing introversion or extraversion tendencies on a scale. The second one looked at the subjects' overt instances of introverted or extraverted behavior, involving (1) the physical distance that the subjects established between themselves and another person or (2) the extent to which the subject initiated conversation. Finally, a target person's ratings of the subject were also possible. Other subjects were led through an identical procedure, but they were asked to respond to *extraversion*-eliciting questions, for example, "What would you do if you wanted to liven things up at a party?"

All of the various measures in the Fazio *et al.* experiment showed the same effect: the subjects given extravert expectations came to act and talk as though they were extraverts, whereas the people handled as introverts moved in the introverted direction. Thus, the indirect social influence—the mere expectation implicit in the introverted and extraverted questions— was sufficient to bring the subjects to characterize themselves as introverts and extraverts, respectively. Their self-knowledge, at least as defined in terms of verbal responses, was thus altered directly by others' expecta- tions. The effects manifested the looking-glass self phenomenon of Cooley (1902): If acquaintances continuously ask us "How long have you been studying? How many books do you own? How many papers do you have your name on?" we begin to get the idea that our social surroundings have defined us as intellectuals, or at least as aspiring ones.

A remarkable facet of the Fazio *et al.* findings was related to the behavioral measure of introversion. To be sure, the subjects came to orient themselves toward others in line with their newly won "self-knowledge." Thus, the procedure resulted in a certain self-labeling (which we are refer- ring to here as an instance of self-knowledge), and in addition, the respon- dents' behavior potentials came to be in line with the labels.

SELF-KNOWLEDGE STEMMING FROM RESISTANCE TO SOCIAL EXPECTATIONS

The relation between indirect social influence and self-knowledge can take an entirely different form. For example, when the social expectation is too strong, individuals who are highly certain about their standing on a given self-dimension can be shown to change *away* from their previous self-conceptions. This idea was formulated and tested in two experiments by Swann, Pelham, and Chidester (1988). In the first study, the subjects were a select sample of women from a southern campus in the United States, all of whom had conservative values about women's roles. We will focus here particularly on the group of women who were highly certain about this value.

The social influence context was reminiscent of that of Fazio *et al.* (1981). In the crucial condition, the subject was asked 10 leading questions, questions that implicitly demanded of the subject that she be more conservative than she actually was: "Why do you think men always make better bosses than women?" "What do you like best about very masculine men?" (Swann *et al.*, 1988, pp. 269, 270). The subjects' immediate verbal responses to these 10 questions were noted, and a questionnaire measure of beliefs about women's roles was then administered. This same measure had been given earlier, so it was possible to note the extent to which the subjects had shifted their conservatism, in one direction or the other. Remarkably, the subjects who were initially certain of their values about women, and who had been confronted with the highly conservatively worded leading questions, changed in the *liberal* direction.

The central aspect of the Fazio *et al.* (1981) and Swann *et al.* (1988) studies for our self-knowledge theme is the following: Just because a person can formulate an answer to the question "How introverted are you?" or "How liberated are you with regard to women's issues?" does not mean that the answer has a firm basis in either deep introspection (self-knower school) or in one's own recent behavior. The relatively subtle effects documented here, which can in no way be called direct influence, suggest that self-knowledge statements may have at their roots subtle ongoing social expectations. If we apply this lesson to the self-disclosure of Jourard (1961, 1968) or to many varieties of therapy approaches, it becomes apparent that the interviewer may be discovering nothing more than the product of subtle social influences, some coming from outside the interview or therapy setting, some taking place within the setting. A cynic would say that casting off previous social facades and expressing the "true kernel of oneself" really amounts to nothing more than altering one's looking-glass self (Cooley) in the direction of more current social expectations (Zurhorst, 1983).

IS THERE MORE TO BUILDING BEHAVIORAL POTENTIAL THAN MERE EXPECTATION?

Our main point has been that the verbal self-description, which is the basis of pronouncements about people's self-knowledge, is a social product. Making such self-oriented statements depends on one's vocabulary of personal descriptors (Benenson & Dweck, 1986; Miller, 1984; Rholes & Ruble, 1984), and the content or direction of those kinds of statements derives from subtle social influences. Among others, expectations from the immediate environment seem to contribute substantially to the form that self-knowledge statements take. In theory, one could limit the study of self-knowledge to the factors that lead a person to use self-descriptors in one way or another. But this limited approach does not take us far enough.

Given that the social milieu provides the raw material for self-descriptions (i.e., among children) and guides self-descriptions in particular directions by means of subtle expectations, there is a point at which these self-ascribed "knowledges" come to function as one's behavior potential. If a person comes to regard himself or herself as a humorist owing to the expectations of others, is there a sense in which this self-regarding or self-defining also steers subsequent actions? Does the person start to tell more jokes? That is of course an issue that bears on the psychology of the internalization of values, attitudes, and personality tendencies. The introversion–extraversion results of the study by Fazio *et al.* (1981) imply that the mere verbal expectation is, in fact, sufficient to set a more-or-less permanent behavioral potential into motion. On the other hand, it is doubtful that any and all social expectations are adequate to establish new behavior potentials. The conditions in which the expectations are communicated may make a telling difference.

In a study by Jones, Rhodewalt, Berglas, and Skelton (1981), discussed in the next section, the broader consequences of a social expectation are examined, this time with the focus on subjects' feelings of self-worth. The subjects were led to act on certain expectations, but the *freedom* with which they could carry out those expectations was varied. The study is thus informative in telling us when an expectation leads to alterations in the person's more general behavioral repertoire or general sense of self-worth.

WHEN SOCIAL EXPECTATIONS PRODUCE MORE THAN PURE SELF-DESCRIPTIONS: THE EFFECT OF FREEDOM

The respondents of Jones *et al.* (1981) were requested to do a favor for the experimenter in the form of acting out the role of a job interviewee. The idea was that the subject would field questions by the interviewer, and the whole session was to be videorecorded.

The "social expectation" in this case was a rather direct one. In one set of conditions, the subject was instructed, "You are to play the role so as to give the interviewer a negative impression of yourself . . . think of yourself on a day when you are really down, when you are in a bad mood" (p. 415). The interview then ensued, and the subjects responded to a series of questions (e.g., "How would you describe your ability to get along with others?") and steered their formulations in a self-abasing direction.

In addition, a variable of free choice was introduced just before the interview. Half the subjects were given a firm directive that they had to play the assigned negative role, and the other half received an explicit opportunity to refuse to carry out the role playing. This choice induction stems from cognitive dissonance theory (Brehm & Cohen, 1962; Festinger, 1957) and has been shown to have a marked impact on respondents' rationalizing uncomfortable or discrepant behaviors. We will return to the meaning of the choice manipulation below.

The interesting measure in this study was an index of self-esteem change. The subjects' self-esteem had been assessed before the study, and following the role playing, self-esteem was measured again, but in such a way that the experimenter ostensibly would not be privy to the scores. The questionnaire was sealed in an envelope, and the subject was asked to take it to a secretary's office, where it would be shipped to another psychologist. Further, the subjects did not put their names on the self-esteem questionnaire.

The social expectation (i.e., the request that the subject play a self-abasing role) was very effective. No matter whether in choice or no-choice circumstances, the subjects carried out the negative role effectively, and Jones et al. found no differences in role-playing behavior during the interview between the choice and the no-choice conditions.

But the important question for us here is "Do the behaviors following from the social expectation have further psychological and behavioral consequences?" And here, the study is very informative. The subjects who played the negative role *without* having choice showed almost no self-esteem change, whereas those given the choice evidenced a decided drop in self-esteem.

The study gives us a hint, in the form of the choice variable, toward answering the question, "When do social expectations produce more than pure self-descriptions?" The instructions to go through the 20-minute interview in a self-derogatory manner were very successful; the subjects were fairly homogeneous in their tendency to display themselves in an unappealing fashion. But when they were removed from the interview context and the social expectations were no longer directly in effect, there was evidence of a certain carryover. If the subjects had a choice in criticizing themselves during the interview, then they showed a corresponding loss in self-esteem.

SOCIAL EXPECTATIONS, CHOICE, AND BEHAVIOR

The theoretical principle underlying the effect just described has a considerable history. It began with the theory of cognitive dissonance (Festinger, 1957; Festinger & Carlsmith, 1959) in a context in which subjects committed "hypocritical" actions. Numerous experiments found that people who made decisions that violated their attitudes or values were especially inclined to rationalize the decision, generally in the form of subjectively upgrading the chosen course of action (Brehm & Cohen, 1962; Wicklund & Brehm, 1976). But "choice" and "chosen" are critical to these effects. Without choice, the person appears to act as though the hypocritical action is already justified; no further rationalization is undertaken.

Aronson and Carlsmith (1963) saw the implications of the theory and paradigm for moral internalization. They undertook a study with children to make a point about choices and internalization of values. The idea was simply this: If a person undertakes a moral action without being forced to do so, and if the action is difficult, involves delay of gratification, or is for other reasons troublesome, the person will then make active efforts to justify the action. The result is an upgrading of the action and of the moral value that the action carries with it. This subjective upgrading then counts as internalization and can be shown to have further behavioral consequences (Axsom & Cooper, 1984; Freedman, 1965; Freedman & Fraser, 1966).

Since the early studies of dissonance theory, the general idea has been extended into a realm called *intrinsic motivation* (Deci, 1975; Deci & Ryan, 1985). The central idea is that a directive from another person, or mere observation of another person, is not sufficient to create a behavioral potential. Although an expectation by others is often sufficient to bring a person to play the role or to make fitting self-descriptions (see the discussion of Jones *et al.* 1981, above), the mere expectation to do something does not seem adequate to bring about internalization. That is, if social expectations are to lead the person to adopt and incorporate a certain form of behavioral potential, then freely carrying out the expectation is the crucial precondition—thus, choice plus action.

This brings us back to the previous chapter and to the experiments by Fazio and Zanna. A consistent feature of their studies was the free action component, in that the self-description (statement of attitude) had a bearing on future behavior only if the attitude could be shown to have a prior behavior base. If subjects formed their attitudes toward five intellectual puzzles simply through passive observation, that attitude had no particular relation to subsequent playing with the puzzles. On the other hand, if the subjects first played with the puzzles, then formed their attitude, the attitude served as a good predictor of what the subjects subsequently did with the puzzles. And in the area of students taking part in psychology experiments, the more experience the subjects had accumulated in psychology experiments, the more their attitudes toward psychology experiments predicted their further participation rate in such experiments (Fazio, 1986).

VERBAL LABELING OF THE SELF AS KNOWLEDGE OF THE SELF: WHAT IS KNOWN, AND WHAT IS NOT KNOWN?

The above discussion leads us in the direction of thinking that two persons must be involved for a full comprehension of the self-knowledge process. Obviously, we need the original self-knowing person, that is, the person who characterizes the self in terms of some behavioral potential (e.g., "I like to participate in psychology experiments" or "I am introverted"). However, if this is the only person involved, the observer or scientist does not understand where such self-knowledges come from. If we are asked directly, "Where does your self-knowledge come from?" the answer is likely to be something of the nature of "From my experiences" or "I should know my own thoughts and values." (To be sure, these are the kinds of statements people make when asked, "What makes you really *you?*" See Andersen, 1984; Andersen & Ross, 1984.) There is no problem in obtaining an answer to "Where does your self-knowledge come from?" from the ostensible self-knower, but such answers are frequently predicated on common sense and have questionable bearing on the actual preceding circumstances, as shown quite convincingly by Nisbett and Wilson (1977b).

But as we have seen above, such self-references, or self-directed labeling, can be shown to stem directly from knowable, controllable, manipulable, observable social circumstances. The person's society makes the labels available through verbal training (Benenson & Dweck, 1986; Bromley, 1977; Miller, 1984; Rholes & Ruble, 1984), and then the society is in the position of bringing the person to one kind of "self-observation" or another, depending on the subtle expectations that are introduced (Fazio *et al.*, 1981). The person whose self-knowledge is of interest is not in a position to judge or recognize these kinds of influences (Bem & McConnell, 1970), and thus, we need a second person—an unbiased observer—in order to understand fully the sources of any particular self-reference.

Suppose that we desire to know (as quasi-scientific observers) whether a particular person has self-knowledge within a given dimension (e.g., introversion-extraversion). We proceed to find out by taking the rather passive route of relying on a questionnaire or a simple interview, and we find that the individual in question is very sure that she is an extravert. Further, a second person is comparatively unsure. Which person has more self-knowledge? Within the context of the present chapter, the question is pointless. All of what the individual maintains in self-references may be the product of (1) good training in the use of the vocabulary of personality and (2) a background of social expectations that steer self-reports in one direction or another.

This is the reason for thinking that two persons must be involved if we are to understand the process. The second person needs to have access to the first person's background in order to calculate where the self-report came from. Was it directly shaped within an environment of strong influence? Was it the product of subtle expectations within the person's environment? These are the kinds of questions that Cooley (1902), Mead (1934), and several contemporary social psychologists would ask. Ultimately, the answer (i.e., to the question, "Where does the self-description begin?") would involve the second person's being able to trace the course of the first person's social background, without having been involved in it, and in sufficient detail so that the statement "I am certain that I am an extravert" can be understood as a product of social influence.

But still more can be known. In the last several pages, we have taken up the issue of the self-description's behavioral consequences, and although the evidence is very sparse, it points unequivocally in the following direction: If a given self-description corresponds to behaviors that the person has previously carried out freely and is not a pure product of social influence, then, in fact, the self-knowledge has a referent. The referent is the behavioral potential. Thus, the second person now has another task, which is to find out whether a given self-description is accompanied by freely undertaken behaviors, behaviors that correspond to the self-description. If this is so, then we are in the position of supposing that the self-knowledge (as indicated by a self-description) is more than just a semantic entity; it is directly tied to a behavioral tendency.

Our conclusion to this chapter is an optimistic one: Self-knowledge, operationalized as self-descriptions or self-labeling, does not have to be seen as a simple verbal repertoire with no accompanying behavioral potential. To be sure, there is no great problem in arranging social circumstances that enhance the person's apparent self-knowledge or that move the manifest self-knowledge in one direction of another. We now have some further basis for knowing when a self-characterization may also correspond to a reliable behavioral tendency. This is, however, not the end of the theoretical possibilities. The next chapter leads us to an even more literal view of self-knowledge and, at the same time, one that has a number of implications for the strength of relation between self-description and the carrying out of actions.

CHAPTER 8

SELF-KNOWLEDGE AS SELF-COGNIZING

This chapter points us in a third direction for coming to terms with self-knowledge. The idea here is, in a sense, simpler than that in the preceding chapter: Self-directed cognitions (or self-directed attention) will be removed from their introspective mystique and placed in a field that we can study empirically. Interestingly, the systematic study of self-cognizing has a long tradition. The tradition has sometimes been broken by decades, but nonetheless, it has a certain continuity. Our look at the topic begins with some ideas that were formulated before the turn of the century.

IN THE CONTEXT OF SUICIDE

Emile Durkheim's book *Suicide* (1897/1957) was a probing analysis of some of the social-psychological roots of suicide (and homicide) in 19th-century Europe. He found, for instance, a higher rate of suicide among Protestants than among Catholics and Jews, differences that he explained with a concept that he termed "egoism." The state of egoism, which was said to be especially high among the Protestants, was described as carrying an element of individual responsibility for one's fate and, simultaneously, a comparative absence of strong group ties. The group that produces egoism, according to Durkheim's argument, is the one that does not govern too many of the person's everyday (and existential) decisions or conflicts. The characteristic Protestants are thus described as people who must function as individuals, who determine their own fate, and whose successes and failures are not really attributable to the group. In contrast, a *well-integrated* religious group, according to Durkheim, keeps its members in check. He thus characterized the Catholic and Jewish groups as providing a solid basis of social support and guidance for a highly ritualized existence, protecting the individual from being overly self-directed.

The analysis was by no means limited to differences in religion. Durkheim also observed suicide differences during times of war and times of peace. Perhaps contrary to common sense, war had a dampening effect on the suicide rate. According to Durkheim, the integration of one's immediate society increases sharply in wartime: common orientations become necessities in time of war and there is no longer the luxury of allowing individuals their self-chosen destinies.

The important psychological facet of egoism, as far as we are concerned, is the negative affect associated with egoism. For Durkheim, this affect was the connection to the suicide rate. Protestants in Durkheim's time did away with themselves more often, periods of peace entailed more suicide, and we are led to think that something about sensing one's individuality is thus connected with a self-critical attitude, a sense of uncertainty or insufficiency. However, Durkheim did not cast himself as a psychologist, and in reading psychological meaning into his interpretations, one is doing a certain amount of speculating. Nonetheless, it seems plausible enough that Durkheim's characteristic Protestants were greater self-cognizers—more attuned to their individuality—than were the active participants in Catholic and Jewish societies.

SELF-CONSCIOUSNESS AND SOCIAL CONTROL

Mead (1934) is rather well known for his theoretical thoughts about taking the role of the other. It was his contention that civilized behavior, thus cooperation and mutual understanding, are mediated by placing oneself mentally in the role of the other. In Mead's language, the "perceptual object of oneself" enables people to anticipate how others will react to them. This mechanism, coming to be aware of oneself in the sense of imaging how others see us, was thought by Mead to underlie the cooperation and lack of total chaos that characterize much of adult behavior.

Shibutani (1961) carried Mead's thinking further, particularly in the sense of specifying the conditions bringing forth such self-consciousness. Correcting a common misconception, Shibutani noted that people are not necessarily chronically "aware of themselves as distinct units" (p. 89). Rather, he considered self-consciousness an acute symptom or phase set off by particular circumstances. What are these circumstances? Did Shib-utani offer us a usable theory about the origins and implications of self-consciousness? Here are some of his examples:

> A person unaccustomed to public speaking who is called upon to address a large group may become so preoccupied with himself that he forgets what he had planned to say.... A person applying for a job may become tongue-tied from paying undue attention to himself. (p. 89)

And some counterexamples, in which there is said to be no self-directed attention:

> When one is absorbed in an exciting motion picture or novel, he is unaware of anything but the development of the plot. His vicarious participation is so complete that he becomes aware of himself only when the drama is over or when something unusual happens to disrupt his concentration. (p. 89)

Shibutani offered us more than vignettes that typify the self-conscious mode of thinking. He proposed more generally that self-consciousness is likely to come about in settings of social participation or mutual depen-dence, but even then, not always: the vital ingredient is an *interference* in ongoing activity, particularly social activities. Should we commit a faux pas or find ourselves on a different wavelength from those with whom we are trying to communicate, self-consciousness is said to be the result.

With Shibutani (1961) we have a strong hint in the direction of a theory about self-knowledge, treated as becoming aware of oneself as an object. Disruptions in social affairs are given as the onset of perceiving oneself as a social object, that is, coming to see oneself as others do.

The remainder of this development can be found in the writings of both Mead (1934) and Shibutani (1961). The outcome of self-consciousness is a self-corrective process:

> Thus, a man becomes conscious of himself as a distinct unit through role-taking; he responds to his own activity as if he were someone else. He responds covertly to his own behavior in the same way in which he expects others to respond overtly. The capacity to form self-images, then, makes self-criticism and self-control possible. (Shibutani, 1961, p. 91)

If we accept Shibutani's hypotheses as a start toward a systematic self-knowledge theory, we must also accept the premise that self-knowledge refers to knowledge of oneself as defined by the perspectives of others. The inward looking to which Mead and Shibutani referred is not the asocial variety that is stressed by the self-knower school. It is just the opposite. The self-criticism that follows the onset of self-consciousness and the beha-vioral adjustments that occur—the controls on impulsive behavior—all come about through self-conscious persons' imagining how others view them.

Shibutani (1961) drew a parallel to Freud in this respect in suggesting that the superego, as a control mechanism, is socially instituted, a mechanism keeping the more individualistic or rudimentary impulses under control. As pointed out by Snyder (1989), a "sense of perceived control about how people are linked to acts provides a predictability that facilitates productive and comfortable group interaction" (p. 147). Self-knowing people for Shibutani are thus the individuals whose attention is momentarily on themselves and who sense the perspectives, the potential approval, and the potential disapproval of others. Self-consciousness or cognizing of the self thus becomes a direct route to self-censure, to self-control, to being a civilized person. Does the person *seek out* such self-conscious experiences? This is an issue not addressed by Shibutani, but it brings us to the next historical element.

FORCING SELF-COGNIZING EXPERIMENTALLY

In a seemingly uncited series of pioneering experiments, Wolff (1932) looked at the psychological impact of induced self-focused attention. Attention to which self? Wolff's interest was exclusively in the aspects that James (1890) referred to as "material," most particularly a person's face, hands, and voice. His subjects were shown pictures of their own facial profiles and their hands, and they also heard recordings of their own voices. Wolff's interest was in the recognition rate, that is, the subjects' ability or willingness to recognize their own features as actually being their own. The outcome, at least in regard to tape-recorded voices, was a profound tendency *not* to recognize one's own voice, that is, to confuse one's voice with that of others. In fact, the subjects recognized their voices with less accuracy than they identified the voices of others.

Although Wolff (1932) did not go into a detailed psychological analysis of these effects, he hinted at an affective process. It is presumably painful to recognize certain self-features, and we may extrapolate from Wolff's observations the notion that self-directed attention is not necessarily sought after, a point that is not explicitly present in Mead's or Shibutani's discussions.

PIECING THE ELEMENTS TOGETHER

From Durkheim, we have the suggestion that unhappiness is related to individuation. The person who is not surrounded by harmonious, supportive, socially stable directives must bear a great deal of responsibility. This condition of individuation, or *egoism*, was seen by Durkheim as the potential basis of destructive behavior, particularly as underlying self-destruction. Similar kinds of affective reactions, especially reactions of aversion or avoidance, were then noted by Wolff (1932) in his empirical work. It is not always the case that self-directed attention is sought after, enjoyed, or tolerated. Then came Mead and Shibutani, with a potential answer to the question, "What self is avoided?" The notion here is that the self that is of interest to psychology is not simply the material self, such as one's body or the sound of one's voice. Rather, the self for the school of symbolic interactionism is the internalized standard, that is, our imagination of how others would respond to us and evaluate us. The others are "symbolic" in that they are carried around in our thoughts; we respond to their wishes or dictates without their being physically present. Much of psychology would refer to such other-based rules as internalized standards.

What are the implications of the above integration? First, we are led in the direction of supposing that self-knowledge can be treated as self-directed attention, as in Wolff's study, in which people heard their own voices. Second, it leads us in the direction of thinking that self-reflection brings the person into a self-evaluative state, one where the internalized values come to be sensed and perhaps also acted on. Third, the thinking of Durkheim and the empirical work of Wolff imply that such self-knowledge is not attractive. Quite aside from its positive (or negative) consequences, self-knowledge of this variety is not necessarily sought after.

In the context of a 1972 statement of a self-awareness theory, Duval and Wicklund tried out various material devices to induce self-directed attention, in a manner not unlike that of Wolff. For instance, subjects' attention was brought to their own facial features or to their own voices by means of confronting subjects with their mirror images or by playing back the sound of their own voices. But the analysis went further: it was proposed that self-directed attention, once induced, then wanders or transfers to those aspects of the person that are salient or prominent in the particular setting. This means, for example, that the sound of their own voices can prompt people to question their moral scruples, if the situation is pertinent to moral issues. Or the sight of their own mirror images could bring individuals to focus on their achievements, if the setting is pertinent to performance.

Certain of James's ideas (1890) are taken very literally here. Self-components are assumed to have an interconnectedness, and once attention is turned to one of them, attention very quickly turns to others to the degree that those others are salient in the situation. The person whose voice is played back via tape recorder is therefore increasingly likely to concentrate on certain behavioral potentials and, more particularly, on those behavioral potentials that are relevant to the setting or that are currently dominant in the person's thinking.

This idea can be presented in more simplified form: If one's attention is steered toward a component of the self, whether toward the material self (James) or directly toward one's behavioral potential, there is an increased readiness to attune oneself to *any* facet of the self. This idea implies, in turn, a method or criterion for knowing whether an individual is, at a given moment, cognizing the self.

SELF-COGNIZING: IS THERE A CRITERION FOR THIS STATE?

Davis and Brock (1975) came up with the idea of an indirect (not introspective) method for checking on the presence of self-directed attention. Their respondents were first confronted with a television camera, or with a mirror, the notion being that the subjects would come to focus on their own physical aspects. Then, the subjects, native English speakers, received a text written in a language unfamiliar to them, where the pronouns were also written in a foreign language unknown to the subjects. It was the subjects' task to guess what the pronouns actually were (in English). Thus, their task was to insert *she, he, their, my,* and so forth at the pronoun points in the text. In addition, a feedback factor was added.

The results showed that the tendency to fill out the text with first-person pronouns increased among subjects who had been confronted with their mirror images or with a television camera. Generally, bringing the subjects to examine their physical features resulted in a readiness to think in terms of the first person. Such results do not indicate what other self-facets (or also self-irrelevant objects) the subjects thought about, but the important point is that a self-connected orientation of a general sort can be induced by means of such simple devices.

Do people always manifest their self-directed thought in such a direct manner? Perhaps the still more important contribution of Davis and Brock was showing what happens after people have had a failure experience. In a separate experimental condition, their subjects encountered a personal failure just before the pronoun procedure, and quite remarkably—but in keeping with Wolff (1932)—the subjects who were confronted with a mirror no longer showed an increment in number of first-person pronouns. Their average number of first-person pronouns was approximately the same as that of subjects in the condition with no mirror or camera.

ATTRIBUTION AND ATTENTION

Duval (1976) and Duval and Wicklund (1973) drew on Gestalt psychology reasoning to arrive at a hypothesis about the direction of attention and the attribution of causality. It was proposed that the individual who is searching for the cause of certain event—at least, a social event—tends to locate causality wherever attention is directed. This implies, for instance, that the direction of attention (inward or outward) would determine whether a person directs causality to the self or not. Duval and Wicklund (1973) presented female subjects with a number of hypothetical situations, such as the following:

> You're driving down the street about 5 miles over the speed limit when a little kid suddenly runs out chasing a ball and you hit him. (p. 22)

Subjects then gave their answers in terms of a "percentage-my-fault" and "percentage-the-child's-fault" format. The experiment showed clearly that self-focused attention, brought about through subjects' looking at themselves in a mirror, increased the extent of self-directed responsibility, in this case by approximately 10%.

This relatively straightforward process, which assumes merely an attention–attribution link, may also be taken as evidence of the direction of someone's attention. Directing responsibility to oneself, including self-blame and self-praise, would appear to be an index of a preexisting attention on the self.

THE PRONOUN INDEX AND A BROADENED ARRAY OF SELF-AWARENESS INDUCERS

The beginning effort of Davis and Brock (1975) was subsequently followed up with further studies showing that other kinds of self-focus inductions do indeed generate a generalized orientation toward the self (see Gibbons, 1990, for an overview). Carver and Scheier (1978) demonstrated that a small audience results in subjects' completing unfinished sentences with more first-person references. In the same context, they showed that people who scored high on a measure of self-consciousness (Fenigstein, Scheier, & Buss, 1975) also evidenced more self-references in responding to incomplete sentences. Using playbacks of subjects' voices, Stephenson and Wicklund (1983) found that subjects who had just heard their own voices were more inclined to use first-person pronouns.

All of this research makes an important point for the ideas to be presented shortly. A simple reminder of some physical aspect of one's own being appears to be sufficient to set off a general inward-directed orientation. But this step is not sufficient for us to talk about self-cognizing as

self-knowledge. We now need to probe into the content of that self-orientation: What is it that the person focuses on (i.e., "knows") in the self-
oriented state?

KNOWING ONESELF: THE SELF-COGNIZING PERSON AS THE CONSISTENT PERSON

The self-knower school has taken us repeatedly in search of the introspective individuals who are supposedly "true to themselves." Inner
harmony, inner consistency, openness to one's actual inner core has been
said to be one of the central defining features of the self-knower.

It is seldom that the self-knower school advances beyond the
definitional stage, and that was the core of the problem sketched out in
Chapter 3. In fact, there were two central problems: First, consistency was
taken as a simple characteristic of the self-knower. No attention was given
to how self-knowledge comes about and how self-knowledge is supposed
to heighten consistency. In other words, consistency was seen as part of the
definition of the self-knower, not as the outcome of systematically inducing self-knowledge. Second, the self-knowledge school has the problem of
defining dimensions of the self. Rather than dealing with consistency in
specific behavioral realms, the self-knower school assumes that a ubiqui-
tous, all-encompassing consistency is an inherent quality of the self-
knower. And we are in strong disagreement with such assumptions.

The present orientation allows us to say something more concrete
about the relation between self-knowledge and its resultant consistency.
Further, this framework allows us to break the self down into specific
components or dimensions, so that enhanced consistency will occur in
certain, salient dimensions but not necessarily in the "entire person." What
does this framework look like?

The theory of Duval and Wicklund (1972) makes the simple assumption that self-focused attention concentrates on whatever dimension is
salient at the moment, such as one's creative potential, one's sociability,
one's tendency to be aggressive, or almost any other behavioral potential.
Second, and important in the present analysis, the theory assumes that
self-directed attention—focused on a particular dimension, such as one's
sociability—will lead the person to strive to eliminate inconsistencies
within that dimension. One of the implications is for the relation between
the actual behavior enacted and one's self-description: a person's self-
description will come to match the actual behavioral tendency if focus is
directed to that dimension.

Accordingly, the idea does not assume that people are chronic self-
knowers (or not), nor does the idea assume that consistency is a wide-

spread characteristic of a whole person. Critical here is self-focus and the dimension that is the object of that focus. Here are some examples.

SOCIABILITY

The first study to try out this thinking was by Pryor *et al.* (1977). Male students were asked to fill out a face-valid 16-item sociability questionnaire. They filled out the questionnaire in a small room, and approximately half of them were seated at a table so that they were confronted with their mirror images. The questionnaire was highly oriented around first encounters with others, particularly encounters with members of the opposite sex (for example, "I feel that I can usually communicate well with members of the opposite sex"). This session was, of course, the critical one theoretically, for it was here that the induction of self-focus should have resulted in the subjects' answering in a way that reflected their actual behavior tendencies. In filling out each question, the self-directed subject should have been attempting to answer so as to reflect overt, habitual modes of responding.

Several days later, the same subjects returned, again individually, and expected to take part in a manual dexterity experiment. They were informed that there would be a brief waiting period before the alleged experiment, and they were then shown to a small room, together with another subject (a female accomplice of the experimenter). The two then sat together for three minutes, so that the subject's overt sociability toward this undergraduate woman could be assessed.

Two methods of looking at actual behavioral sociability were used. In one method, the woman was instructed to form an overall impression of the subject's sociability during the three-minute period and to make a final rating after the interaction. The other method consisted simply of the number of words spoken by the subject to the woman, recorded with a tape recorder. These two indices related highly to each other, and they were combined into a single behavioral measure of sociability.

Interestingly, there was not much sign of self-knowingness in the control (i.e., non-self-aware) condition: The correlation between the sociability scale score and the subsequent behavior was a very low .16. The value is insignificant and points to a lack of the subjects' reporting anything in line with their behavioral potential in sociability. The correlation in the self-aware condition was .62,* showing that the self-aware subjects

---

*The experiment was carried out twice, under nearly identical conditions. The first time the experiment was conducted, the control and mirror-condition correlations were .03 and .55, respectively. The second time, the values were .28 for the control condition and .73 for the mirror condition. The values reported here in the text involve all of the data taken together and are also to be found in Wicklund (1975).

were doing something rather significant when confronted with the mirror. Although it was not possible to ask the subjects about their actual cognitive processes while filling out the scale, we may surmise that they were trying to answer so as to create a correspondence between their answers and their usual behavioral tendencies. Their responses, seen from the angle of the present chapter, were self-knowing responses, that is, accurate responses as measured against overt tendencies. The sociability phenomenon is not an isolated phenomenon, and we might have a look at further illustrations of this truth-telling process.

INTELLIGENCE

One's behavioral potential does not always have to be assessed through an ongoing behavioral stream, as for example, one's actions in a social scenario. Potential can also be indicated through ability tests, and more concretely, it is safe to say that one's potential for language-related performance and mathematics-related performance is measurable via standard college-aptitude tests. A person who scores high is likely to obtain higher grades in the areas that are tested.

North American college students characteristically take such tests and of course are aware of their results before beginning college. This circumstance allows us to examine a certain rudimentary kind of self-knowledge: To what degree is the person capable of recalling that score, and is it distorted upward? Interestingly, there appears to be a general upward distortion, but especially among students whose objective scores are low, as will be shown shortly. The theoretically interesting issue is the extent to which self-knowledge, in the sense of self-cognizing, can bring the individual to align the self-report with the objective fact.

The study that addresses this issue was also carried out by Pryor *et al.* (1977). It was possible to obtain the Scholastic Aptitude Test (SAT) score of each participant, and the participants were divided into two groups: those with relatively high SAT scores (i.e., scores falling above the median of the distribution) and those with lower scores.

The participants, all male students, appeared for the experiment individually. The experimenter (one of two women served as experimenter) explained that she was looking at some of the traits associated with the subject's choice of a major, and in line with this purpose, she had prepared a brief questionnaire. The subject was then ushered into a small room and seated at a table. Half the subjects were confronted with a mirror while seated at the table; for the other half, there was no mirror. The questionnaire that was administered contained the crucial item, which was the subject's own statement of his verbal-plus-quantitative Scholastic Aptitude Test score.

The results of this procedure were very clear. There was an overall effect of self-focused attention, so that the presence of the mirror brought subjects to align their self-descriptions with the objective fact. This effect was most pronounced among the students whose actual scores were low. Without self-awareness-inducing circumstances, they reported their scores at an average level of 78 points above their true level; with the induction of self-awareness, this distortion shrunk to 22.9 points above the actual level. And among those whose actual obtained scores were high, the distortion shrunk to a mere 7.7 points.

Again, one sees that these increments in self-report accuracy were not part of a general, continuing self-knowingness. Rather, a person who was generally apt to exaggerate his SAT score greatly was also capable of bringing the self-report into line with objective reality. *Self-knowledge* in this context meant only that attention came to be focused on the self, initially on one's physical being via the mirror, and then on the specific dimension involved in the self-report. Such increments in consistency were not the product of long-term training or of a specific type of introspective personality; rather, they reflected the momentary focus of attention on a specific dimension of behavioral potential.

THE LOGICAL INFERENCE OF ATTITUDE FROM BEHAVIOR

Understanding oneself does not refer exclusively to self-aspects that have always been in one's behavioral repertoire. Borrowing from self-perception theory (Bem, 1972) and from the work of Fazio and Zanna (1978), we can also talk about the formation of a potentially chronic behavioral tendency. The idea is that a freely enacted behavior—a decision or a series of decisions—can produce a readiness to enact that same behavior again. And further, to the extent that the behavior is salient or vivid for the person, self-descriptions are likely to be made consistent with that newly enacted behavioral sequence.

If a person has just enacted a behavior for the first time—for instance, in an exploratory situation—and is then asked for an opinion about that behavior, self-cognizing should lead to an increase in consistency between the self-report (opinion) and the act. For instance, when the subject is asked how attractive or interesting the action is, consistency would mean basing attractiveness on the actual frequency with which the act is performed.

The third experiment reported by Pryor *et al.* (1977) looked at this possibility within an extremely simple situation. Each of the subjects, female undergraduates, was given five paper-and-pencil problems to work on. They were labeled "letter series, cube comparison, Gestalt completion, hidden figures, and nearer point." All of them were soluble. The subject was given an ample supply of each of the five problem types and was told to try them out for 10 minutes. The experimenter emphasized that the situation was free, in that the subject was to work on any of the types for as long as she desired.

Following the 10-minute work period, each subject had developed an implicit hierarchy of preferences through her behaviors. Even though most of the problems had never been encountered by subjects previously, the subjects now had a behavioral base for making statements about their preferences among the five problem types.

In the second part of the study, the subject was brought to a small room, either with a mirror mounted on the table or not. The subject was handed a questionnaire on which the five types of problems were to be rated on a scale of "extremely boring" to "extremely interesting." The ratings were made on a scale running from –5 to +5. In order to calculate consistency, the extent to which each problem type was worked (during the foregoing 10-minute period) was correlated with the rating that the problem received. For each subject, a correlation was then computed, and these correlations were averaged. In the control (no-mirror) condition, there was very little evidence of a consistency effect; the correlation was a mere .13. In other words, the mere fact of having behaved is evidently not sufficient to prompt the person to draw a corresponding conclusion about the attractiveness of the problems. In the self-awareness condition, the correlation rose to a significant .74, which means that, if a subject worked a particularly high number of the "nearer point" problems, then that problem was rated as highly interesting.

We can see on the basis of these three experiments that the induction of self-focus results in a self-knowledge in the form of consistency. The consistency here came into being through guiding the subject's verbal report in the direction of an objective behavioral potential, and the three studies show that this process appears to function no matter what form the behavioral potential takes. It can be a long-standing personality disposition, such as sociability; it can be a test score that reflects one's capacities; or it can be a newly acquired behavioral repertoire, as in the simple preferences among paper-and-pencil games.

Chronic Self-Cognizing

How does the self-cognizing process work with individuals who, for whatever reason, tend to be more chronically attuned to themselves? One method of looking at this issue is by using a scale of self-direction that has come to be regarded as a standard instrument. This is the "private" self-consciousness scale of Fenigstein *et al.* (1975). The scale uses rather straightforward questions in order to get at whether individuals tend, across situations, to be cognitively oriented toward themselves.

Scheier *et al.* (1978) used this scale as the starting point in a study that looked at the consistency of subjects' reports about their own hostility and thus, presumably, their predisposition to aggressive or hostile behavior (Buss & Durkee, 1957). As the starting point for the study, it was necessary to ask each subject to fill out both the self-consciousness scale and the hostility inventory. Then, in a laboratory setting, Scheier *et al.* tested each subject's propensity to act out physically against others, in the form of subjects' readiness to administer shock to a target person.

There was no average difference between the high and low self-aware subjects, a finding indicating that self-awareness *per se* does not determine the person's absolute level of aggression or hostility. However, when we examine the relation between the shock level administered and the subject's hostility score, the interesting differences emerge. Among the low self-focus subjects (as assessed by the self-consciousness scale), the correlation between the hostility score and the amount of shock given was scarcely above zero (i.e., .09). But the subjects who were chronically highly self-focused manifested a hostility–shock correlation of .66.

Let us recapitulate the reasoning behind this finding. First of all, the respondents were questioned regarding their presumed long-lasting self-consciousness. The scale allows us to divide the people into comparatively high (and low) self-focused groups. This does not mean that the subjects in the two groups were "by their nature" self-oriented or less self-oriented; it might also mean, for example, that one group was more regularly exposed to circumstances that fostered self-focus. For instance, these subjects may more often have been the object of others' attention; they may have been singled out more often than the others (see Duval, 1976); or their possible lack of social interaction may have led to less deindividuation (Diener, 1979). Whatever the reason, however, these individuals were evidently higher in self-focus, at least at the time of the empirical study.

At the moment of filling out the scale, the dimension of hostility or aggression was made salient to the subject, and we are assuming here that the general tendency to be self-focused transferred to the specific dimension in question. Therefore, the people who had a high value on the self-consciousness scale now came to focus on their own hostility and, in the course of doing so, adjusted their self-reports so that they were consistent with the ongoing behavioral tendency. This behavioral tendency was then tapped into by finding out how much shock the subjects were inclined to give another person, and just as in the study of sociability (above), the person's verbal statement came to match the ongoing potential. This is, then, an example of how self-knowledge can be treated within the framework of cognizing of the self. The simple focus of attention is sufficient to bring about a valid reflection on self-components. But our analysis does not end with this point; there is considerably more that can be said about these facets of self-knowledge.

SELF-COGNIZING AND ACTING ON INTERNALIZED STANDARDS

An important aspect of our introduction to this chapter is the analysis of Mead (1934), from whom we derive the notion that others' perspectives come to be incorporated into our own worldview. More simply stated, through taking the perspectives of others toward us, we come to treat their perspectives as an integral part of us. Internalization of others' values, attitudes, or other norms for behavior have, of course, been treated from a variety of theoretical standpoints. According to Hoffman (1977), internalization proceeds by way of differential memory. Children are exposed to their parents' way of seeing things, thus to the parents' values and attitudes, and gradually forget that the parents were associated with those attitudes. As a result, children eventually conclude that the values originate in themselves. In turn, they are more ready to act on these values outside the family context.

Another mode of analysis, showing up primarily in the work on intrinsic motivation (Deci & Ryan, 1985) and cognitive dissonance theory (Aronson & Carlsmith, 1963), regards the internalization of others' values as a process of acting on the values without being forced to do so. Within the dissonance theory approach, this free acting on a value results in the person's rationalizing having done so, with the result that the value is built up (made more positive) within the person's repertoire of values. In turn, this process increases the likelihood of the person's implementing the value later.

ASK DIRECTLY? OR ASSUME THAT IT IS ALREADY THERE?

Although it is plausible that internalization takes place, we need to know something more in order to implement the self-cognizing ideas. That is, we need to know whether any given individual has, in fact, internalized a particular attitude or value. How do we go about this? The only method that is certain is to look at the person's actual consistency *outside* the context in which the value was first learned or internalized. This means that we have to know about both the person's social background, meaning the values to which the person has been exposed early, and the person's acting on those values later. This is an imposing research endeavor, and thus far, in the research we shall report, the approach has been somewhat more modest.

In fact, two alternatives have been taken. The one assumes that almost all members of a given group or subpopulation represent a particular value, that is, that it has been internalized. The self-focus induction and measurement of value-consistent behavior proceeds from that point. The second alternative begins on a more fine-grained level and asks each individual respondent for the idiosyncratic value or attitude. We can now proceed to see how the self-focus approach to self-knowledge comes to terms with the above issues.

HONESTY IN EXAM TAKING: A WIDESPREAD NORM AMONG STUDENTS

Diener and Wallbom (1976) presented their subjects with a wonderful opportunity to cheat. They were given an intelligence test with a definite time limit and were requested not to exceed this limit. They were then left alone in the room to perform as best they could and as fast as they could. Were these students basically against cheating? Diener and Wallbom reported statistics indicating that about 90% of American college students claim to be opposed to cheating on tests. This is, then, a hint that their subjects may well have been carrying this value.

Half the subjects performed the IQ test in the presence of a mirror, and half without a mirror, and it was possible to record whether the subjects cheated, in the sense of working beyond the given time limit. Remarkably enough, 71% of the subjects cheated when no self-awareness induction was present, which would almost make us think that most of the subjects were hypocrites, not really having internalized the norm of not cheating. Quite remarkably, the percentage of cheaters dropped to 7% when the test was carried out in the presence of the mirror.

The results give us a strong hint about the role of self-knowledge—defined as self-cognizing—in bringing the internalized cultural value into play in behavior. On a verbal level, the students were certainly prepared to claim that they were opposed to cheating on exams, but their cheating behavior indicated that the incentive value of attaining a high score seemed to make them inattentive to their ostensibly internalized values. The forcing of self-focus broke up this hypocrisy and brought the subjects' behavior back into line with the internalized norm. Again, a notable feature of these phenomena is the sudden switch—from a hypocritical, seemingly non-self-knowing individual, to a consistent person, controlled by the internalized dictates of the group or society.

PUNITIVENESS IN TEACHING

Instead of making a blanket assumption about all individuals representing a given societal norm, we can also think in terms of each person's idiosyncratic value system, on the assumption that we are drawing people from heterogeneous backgrounds. One case in point is punitiveness in teaching, a theme that was the subject of two studies by Carver (1975). Carver began by giving each subject a short scale that tapped into the subject's thoughts about punishment in teaching, focusing particularly on the idea that punishment facilitates learning. As expected, there was considerable variation among subjects, and Carver divided his sample into people who were clearly against punishment as a tool in teaching and people who were definitely in favor of punishment.

When the subjects came to the laboratory, they found themselves in the role of a teacher. Their "pupil" was supposed to learn verbal concepts, and each time the pupil gave an incorrect answer, the subject-teacher was supposed to administer an electric shock. This procedure, modeled after the prototype of Buss (1961), allowed the measurement of the intensity of shocks administered.

Each of the two groups—low-punitive and high-punitive—was further subdivided into self-aware and control conditions. In the self-aware condition a mirror was mounted so that subjects could see their faces, as well as their hands moving the shock levers. Carver simply averaged the intensities of shock delivered over the course of the learning trials, and the results in the no-mirror group reflected no difference whatever between the groups that were categorized as high-punitive and low-punitive. Similarly to the findings of Diener and Wallbom, the subjects appeared to be hypocrites, as measured against their stated values about punishment. A person whose verbal statement on the questionnaire indicated a punitive approach to learning showed, in fact, no more actual punishment than did someone whose values were lenient.

The simple confrontation with the mirror image altered this picture considerably. The high-punitive group then became significantly *more* punitive in terms of shock intensity, and the low-punitive group's shock level tended to drop. The results of this and of a second, highly similar experiment by Carver (1975) make the point that self-cognizing does not simply increase the intensity of one's response or exaggerate tendencies that are present in the particular experimental setting. Rather, a certain background of the subject is brought to the fore in terms of behavior. Self-knowledge, as defined in this context, thus led both to more aggression and to somewhat less aggression, depending on what had previously been internalized.

ENJOYING OR REPUDIATING PORNOGRAPHY

A considerable variation among individuals can also be expected when we turn to such issues as puritanism, repressive attitudes, or, in this case, sex guilt. A series of studies by Gibbons (1978) again takes the route of examining respondents' values, and then finding out about behavior–value consistency through giving the person an opportunity to manifest the value. In Gibbons's paradigm, female participants read a passage from a pornographic novel and then rated their enjoyment of the novel. The consistency in this case was consistency between the subject's statement of her sex guilt, a rather broad or far-reaching value, and her specific evaluative reaction to the pornographic literature.

The procedure worked this way: In an initial testing session, the female student subjects filled out a sex guilt scale (Mosher, 1968), which had been modified by Langston (1973). A characteristic item was, "Sex relations before marriage (a) ruin many a happy couple . . . (b) are good in my opinion" (Gibbons, 1978, p. 981). After the subjects had filled out the scale, Gibbons selected for use in the actual experiment subjects with relatively high sex-guilt scores as well as a group with low sex-guilt scores.

The subjects were assigned to a room that had no self-awareness-inducing devices (control condition) or to a room with a mirror. Among other tasks, the subjects were asked to read a passage that had been adapted from a pornographic novel, and immediately thereafter, they were asked to rate the literary passage on the dimensions "sexually arousing," "enjoyable," and "well written."

What should we expect from this procedure? A subject who indicates a good many misgivings about sexual goings-on—disapproval of extramarital sex, a questioning attitude toward the propriety of sexually permissive literature, and, more generally, a puritanical point of view—would be expected to rate the pornographic material unfavorably. In order to have a combined index of the subjects' reaction to the passage, Gibbons combined the individual measures ("sexually arousing," "enjoyable," "well-written") into a single evaluative index and then looked at this overall evaluation relative to the subjects' initial sex-guilt scores.

Once again, there was very little apparent consistency within the control condition. The correlation between the sex guilt score and the later evaluation of the pornography was almost exactly zero (actually, $-.02$), again showing that people do not automatically evidence their expressed values in settings where the value can potentially be implemented. In the self-focus condition, the corresponding correlation was .71, an unusually high degree of correspondence between value and subsequent reaction.

CREATIVITY

Creative responding can be regarded, in part, as directed toward one's ideals regarding creativity or uniqueness. Even though there may well be upper limits on one's creative possibilities, we may also assume that the motivation to be creative makes a sizable difference in the end product of one's efforts. This motivation may, of course, be enhanced through the individual's trying to reach standards that have been internalized. Just as in the preceding research on punitiveness and sex guilt, we should expect self-focus to bring participants' efforts into line with their individual values.

Hormuth (1982) carried this line of thinking into an experiment that began with assessing values about creativity. Based on a measure by Scott (1965), Hormuth selected male subjects who were either in the upper quartile or the lower quartile in terms of creative values. Then, three to eight weeks later, these subjects came to the laboratory, and the behavioral index of creativity was measured: First of all, the subjects learned associations between a set of 10 common words and a further set of corresponding pairs. For instance, if *long* was the stimulus word, the word to be associated with it was *short*. Or if *bitter* was the stimulus word, its paired associate was *sweet*. The subjects were taught these 10 common associations so that they could quite easily repeat the paired associate when the stimulus word was presented.

Then came the second phase, during which originality was assessed behaviorally. The subjects were told, "Now this time you'll see a word come up in the first window, and I want you to give a response to this word. It can either be a previously learned response or a creative, original response, and there is no right or wrong answer" (Hormuth, 1982, pp. 36–37). This was, then, the opportunity for the subjects to come up with an unusual, relatively original association. For instance, instead of responding to *warm* with *cold*, one might answer *boiling*. Although the reader may be reluctant to accord such an answer the status of creativity, this is about the best that one can do within the constraints of measurable responses, and to be sure, Hormuth saw to it that the responses classified as unusual were indeed objectively unusual: Based on the Palermo and Jenkins (1964) list of word associations, each response of the subject received a score along the dimension of "usual-unusual," and the data were treated so that an original (unusual) response received a high score.

The manipulation was similar to those used in the foregoing experiments, in that half of the subjects were confronted with their mirror images during the crucial phases of the study. In the group that indicated high creativity on the paper-and-pencil measure, self-focus increased original responding markedly. In the group that was low in scale-defined creativity, there was a slight tendency to become *less* original when confronted with the mirror.

IS IT ALL A FACADE?

A certain uneasiness develops when one tries to examine these findings through the perspectives of the self-knower school. The self-knowing person is cast as a stable entity; self-knowers are supposed to be people who have developed themselves, who have "found" themselves, who are not at the mercy of the whims or vicissitudes of the social setting. The self-knower is said to be *generally* consistent; the self-knower is tolerant, not punitive, not laden with sex guilt. The picture that we have created here does not fit well with that of the self-knower school, primarily in two respects:

1. Self-knowledge as dealt with here is a short-lived phenomenon. It comes and goes as a function of the self-focusing power of one's circumstances, and its impact depends on which particular self-aspect is salient.

2. Self-knowledge, as self-focusing, can draw out the person's potential in *any* respect, so that self-cognizing results not just in behaviors that fit the self-knower school portrait (e.g., warmth and creativity), but also behaviors that run counter to that idealized image, that is, punitiveness in teaching (Carver, 1975) and puritanical leanings (Gibbons, 1978).

The nonfit between the conception of this chapter and that of the self-knower school can be summarized adequately by noting that the traditional self-knower as viewed by the self-knower school is a stable entity and, equally important, manifests certain characteristics that are indicative of self-knowledge. The objection of the self-knower school to the approach of this chapter would thus have to be something like this: The present research is looking only at the superficial, changeable self. In order to get at *real* self-knowledge, one has to seek more deeply. But let us have a careful look at the meaning of *deep*. How do we embark on this search?

"DEEPER SELF" CHARACTERISTICS

We might try the criteria of Jourard (1961). Healthy, self-insightful individuals do a great deal of talking about themselves. Self-references, confessions, references to their problems—all of these are ostensibly indicative of self-insight and absence of neuroticism. Likewise, in Rogers (1950, 1951, 1961), expressing feelings, shunting aside the cognitive-ana-lytical form of expression, and being open to feedback—these all indicate that the person is on the road to self-insight. The self-knower school assumes a certain permanence in this self-insight; once attained, it does not easily slip away. And the self-knower school assumes a strong generality of such self-insight. Possession of self-knowledge means that we are self-knowing in all respects; the knowledge is not limited to compartmen-talized aspects of ourselves.

This approach, the spotting of the right characteristics, is the only way that the self-knower school proceeds to study self-knowledge. There is no direct analysis of the person's cognitions; there is no consideration of the person's attention. Rather, "deep" self-knowledge is defined in terms of a certain communication style, the very style depicted by Jourard and Rog-ers. And here is the difficulty. Readiness to talk about oneself, openness to feedback about oneself, the appearance of warmth, and related character-istics are not necessarily any more than a learned communication style. The statement "I feel that I am an altruistic person," as opposed to "I am an altruistic person," is a learned expression; it is the product of civilizing influences. One can hardly argue that the tendency to say "I feel" stems directly from having contact with one's deeper self.

Consistency

The same kinds of problems arise when we look at the more specific personal characteristics that are said to reflect self-knowingness, such as consistency. If a person's self-descriptions are in line with others' descrip-tions of that person, consistency (and self-knowledge) is presumed to be high. Such consistency is said to reflect deeper insights into oneself. But what is the underlying logic? Is it to be assumed that both persons and their observers have direct access to some deeper self-kernel? The simple analysis of these kinds of consistencies says simply that the person's self-descriptions are a product of the social environment that shapes those self-descriptions (see Fazio et al., 1981); in fact, such consistencies may come into being without the person's having any sense of self whatever.

In short, the objection (that the self-cognizing research treats only the facadelike, temporary self) is not compelling, as we see no possibility of understanding what might be meant by a "deeper, asocial self." In fact, the indicators of the "true" self suggested within the self-knower school may easily be the product of social influence, and in no way do they have to indicate actual reflection on or perception of one's behavioral potential.

SELF-INSIGHT INTO BODILY FUNCTIONING

One aspect of the self-knower school argument takes us in the direction of the inner self in the sense of the person's bodily functioning. It is argued simply that bringing patients' or research subjects' thoughts to their internal functioning, and away from social influences (i.e., the self as a social product), will result in deeper self-knowledge.

How does this process work in detail? The primary difficulty of the self-knower school is in its absence of psychological variables. We do not know what brings a person to comprehend or perceive internal functioning, that is, perceive directly when one is aware or tired, when adrenaline is flowing, and the like. Rather, the idea is simply that, *however it comes about, through therapy or otherwise, a knowledge of the body's internal functioning will override the obedience to social norms or other forms of social pressure.* This is an interesting hypothesis, but there is no evidence for it. And further, there is no evidence to support the idea that "self-knowers," as indicated by the frequency of self-relevant remarks or the degree of humanistic leanings, have a more fine-tuned sense of what goes on within their bodies.

On the other hand, there is a possible route to looking at knowledge of one's physiological variables, and this takes us once again to the main theme of this chapter.

SELF-COGNIZING DIRECTED TO BODILY STATES

At this juncture, we will take the ideas about self-cognizing in a different direction, and instead of applying the idea to internalized social standards, we will deal with the cognizing of bodily effects. There is, as above, no assumption here that any given individual is particularly gifted (or inept) in perceiving physiological changes accurately. Rather, the approach assumes only that self-focused attention, and the salience of a given physiological aspect, will result in the person's more concentrated attention on that aspect.

REDUCED SUSCEPTIBILITY TO PLACEBOS

The first effort to relate general self-focus to physiological functioning was reported by Gibbons, Carver, Scheier, and Hormuth (1979). Among the subjects who were administered a placebo, along with instructions regarding the likely effects of the "medication," there was generally a tendency to report experiencing the suggested effects. However, the subjects who found themselves confronted with their mirror images during the critical phases of the procedure did not report the suggested symptoms. It was as though they were no longer confused by the suggestion, in that their self-focus led them to a more veridical perception of their physiological changes or lack of changes. A similar effect was found by Gibbons and Gaeddert (1984), in a context in which the drug was said to have an inhibiting or facilitating effect on performance. Attribution to the drug (which was in fact only baking soda) was greater among non-self-focused subjects, whereas the self-focused group evidenced a quite accurate sense of their actual arousal.

HEARTBEAT DISCRIMINATION

In an intriguing experiment by Weisz, Balazs, and Adam (1988), subjects followed a procedure that called on their sense of their own heartbeat. They were presented with a series of tones, some of which coincided, and others of which did not coincide, with their own heartbeat. These different tones may be labeled "true heart-rate feedback" and "false heart-rate feedback":

> They were instructed to respond "yes" if they considered the rhythm of the tones to be identical with the rhythm of their present heartbeats, and "no" if not. . . . Subjects were never provided with knowledge of results. (p. 195)

The results of the comparison of a mirror condition versus a no-mirror condition showed a decidedly superior performance by the self-focused subjects. The mirror seems to have resulted in the subjects' sensing more accurately the pace of their own heart rate.

THE DEEP SELF OR THE SOCIAL FACADE?

The preceding empirical work shows that self-cognizing, as set off in a general manner through sitting in front of a mirror, can lead the person temporarily to a heightened sensitivity to physiological processes. The subjects were less likely to be duped by instructions regarding the physiological impact of a placebo and were more able to discriminate sounds reflecting their heart rate from sounds not reflecting their heart rate. In short, self-focus would appear to heighten one's attunement to salient physiological processes.

But here is the issue for the self-knower school: Does a person's sensitivity to inner, asocial physiological events imply a corresponding rejection of the "social facade"? Probably not, if we take a quick review of the foregoing research directions. The studies we discussed at the beginning of this chapter demonstrated that self-cognizing results in the person's acting on internalized social values. For some people, the internalized value may be punitive; for others, nonpunitive. And it would be a fair assumption that one and the same person can undergo "self-knowledge" in both of these respects, that is, in terms of both more acute perception of one's own physiology and a greater reactivity to the social norms that stem from one's background.

PSYCHOLOGICAL HEALTH AND PHYSIOLOGICAL FUNCTIONING

One cannot take the attention of the self-knower school away from the simplistic thesis that lots of self-related thought and a "healthy" amount of self-oriented verbiage will have favorable effects on the individual's psychological and physical condition. Nowhere in the writings of this school do we see any exceptions to the idea that attunement to the self brings health, in every respect. Perhaps so, but let us look at the pertinent research on self-focused cognitions to see whether other kinds of effects are imaginable.

For one thing, it seems clear that self-focused attention is not desired and is thus avoided when a person has just experienced a failure or has committed hypocrisy. Experiments by Duval, Wicklund, and Fine (in Duval & Wicklund, 1972), Gibbons and Wicklund (1976), and Greenberg and Musham (1981) make this point explicit. For instance, experimental subjects who have just received unfavorable feedback regarding their creativity and IQ are more likely to avoid their mirror images than people who have received favorable feedback (Duval *et al.*, in Duval & Wicklund, 1972). Similarly, subjects who have acted hypocritically are strongly apt to avoid sitting before a mirror, relative to subjects who have engaged in value-consistent behavior (Greenberg & Musham, 1981). Given such avoidance tendencies, does it follow that forced self-focus will lead to psychological and physical health? If anything, one might suppose that the result would be stress, further humiliation, lowered self-esteem (see Brockner & Hulton, 1978), and the like.

Right to the point is a research program by Pyszczynski, Holt, and Greenberg (1987), which demonstrated (1) that a relatively high level of self-focus accompanies depressive symptoms, and (2) that getting depressed subjects to focus their attention externally serves to alleviate the depressive tendencies. With respect to the latter point, Pyszczynski *et al.* asked all participants to write a short story, following a technique developed by Fenigstein and Levine (1984). Half the subjects were asked to use as many terms as possible from a list containing such words as *I, mirror, alone,* and *me,* and the external-focus subjects were asked to draw on a list containing such words as *he, picture, together,* and *him* (p. 998). The dependent measure asked the subjects about the probability of their subsequently experiencing negative or positive events (such as "not finding a job" or "traveling to Europe"). The results indicated clearly that the externally focused, as opposed to self-focused subjects, were more optimistic about their future. This pattern of results was equally strong no matter whether the subjects were initially depressed or nondepressed.

Also in the clinical realm, the potentially damaging consequences of self-focused attention have been recognized. Beginning with a survey of Adler's work, Wallach and Wallach (1983) reviewed a number of clinical perspectives that cope with neuroses from the standpoint that the client is overly self-centered or self-focused. For example:

> Over a number of years, Frankl has argued that a great deal of therapy, quite the opposite of what is needed, in effect invites the neurotic to focus more attention on his or her own feelings and sensations. (p. 234)

Wallach and Wallach also referred to the psychiatrist William Glasser, who similarly found that a self-focusing route to therapy only exacerbates the problem. Still another psychotherapist, Morita Shoma, also emphasized the redirection of attention to outside events. The connection to the research of Pyszczynski *et al.* is clear.

One can extend the self-focus and health theme into the realm of cardiovascular complaints. In a novel research program, Scherwitz, Graham, and Ornish (1985) examined the relation between self-references, the Type A syndrome (which can be construed as a propensity to heart problems), and actual heart disease. Within a student sample, Scherwitz *et al.* found that Type A respondents used approximately twice as many self-references as their Type B counterparts within a context in which the students related an incident that had made them angry. In a subsequent study, the authors studied a sample of men who evidenced abnormal exercise electrocardiograms, and among these, the correlation between the number of self-references and blood pressure was an impressive .70. Still more dramatically, Scherwitz *et al.* looked at actual heart disease, this time including both the variables A/B Type and smoker/nonsmoker. Among smokers, the frequency of self-references contributed to heart attacks, and among extreme Type A individuals, self-involvement had a very marked disadvantageous effect as measured in terms of heart problems.

An interesting sidelight of these results is a breakdown of the kinds of self-references that predicted especially well. The pronoun *my* was outstanding in this respect, and Scherwitz *et al.* conjectured that

> "my" acts to extend the self outward toward possessions, reflecting one's attachment to various aspects of the environment. . . . The more we possess, the

more there is to protect and control, thereby increasing our sense of vulner-
ability. (p. 14)

The implication of this research for the self-focus health thesis is clear
enough. Self-focus, self-preoccupation, and the like do not automatically
spell an enlargement of one's general self-knowledge in the sense of coming into contact with the real and stable self. The self-awareness research
reported above demonstrates that self-focus brings the person's behavior
into line with societal standards and results in a close fit between behaviors
and internalized standards, and the line of thought just summarized
shows that self-awareness processes are accompanied by avoidance tendencies and even by unwanted psychological and physiological consequences. A fair summary statement of the self-focus research is that the
individual is brought under societal control, and further, that the individual's well-being does not automatically improve as a result.

SELF-COGNIZING AND THE SALIENCE OF SELF-ASPECTS

We have no basis whatever for imagining that those who are in a
phase of self-cognizing attend more to the physiological "kernel" of themselves than to social norms. In fact, the issue of whether attention is more
on physiological aspects or more on social factors is meaningless within
the context of this chapter, for the simple reason that self-focus can bring
the person's attention to bear on *any* element of the self. Where attention
focuses and has an effect depends quite simply on the aspects that are
salient. People can be more "in touch" with their physiological functioning
or more in touch with socially instigated norms, depending on the salience
of these aspects at the moment.

One of the lessons of the research here is that self-knowledge should
best be treated as the momentary cognizing of a given self-dimension, for
the simple reason that a given dimension does not remain indefinitely in
the focus of one's insightful powers. As the research of Carver (1975),
Gibbons (1978), and Hormuth (1982) demonstrates, a person can on some
occasions be a hypocrite, in the sense of not acting on incorporated values,
and at other times a highly consistent, "moral" person, one who adheres
closely to internalized social standards. The fantasy persons of the self-
knower school—that is, the individuals who have pushed aside society's
influences in favor of their "own" superior manner of going about
things—are people who have not yet been discovered in research. And of
course, the difficulty in that conception lies in trying to define *own*. Values
and standards do not stem directly from physiology, and were a person to
overthrow previously incorporated values successfully, it is a fair guess

that a new set would be adopted (Zurhorst, 1983). Additionally, we see no basis for supposing that self-orientation will automatically engender psychological or physical health. If anything, the self-focused state is one in which self-esteem is threatened, depression is deepened, the self-focused state is avoided, and certain physical ailments are exacerbated. In speaking of the self-aware person, we may talk of one who is societally controlled, but not necessarily better off for being controlled.

CHAPTER 9

SELF-KNOWLEDGE VIEWED IN A SYMBIOTIC RELATIONSHIP

THE NEED TO CONTROL MEETS THE READINESS TO BE CONTROLLED

THE OSTENSIBLE BENEFITS OF SELF-KNOWLEDGE TO SOCIETY

Once again turning to the self-knower school, we are led to imagine that self-knowledge is of unquestionable value both to society and to the individual who is in possession of it. Self-knowledge and other concepts closely allied to it point to the autonomous, self-determined individual, whose democratic thinking, tolerance, altruism, and consistency are the traits in which the society surrounding the self-knower school is interested. On the other hand, as the development of the self-knower is described, the process entails the shunting aside of all social influence and of not allowing one's values to be defined or dictated by others, and instead of possessing just a repository of societal influences, the individual is supposed to arrive at a true, inner core. This all sounds very selfish, antisocial, and egoistical, as though it would be coupled with vanity or autism in its extreme forms. But the self-knower school's counterargument is also a straightforward one: The inner core that is discovered in the self-insight process is ultimately a core that is common to all individuals;

thus, when discovered, it allows the person a highly prosocial repertoire and furthers social relations very positively.

The self-knower position floats on a rather nonscientific level and is also one that can easily be called into question, as indicated above. The purpose of this chapter, however, is more concrete: Our interest is in society's control over the hero, the ostensible self-knowing person, and we want to treat two aspects of this control.

The first issue deals directly with the self-knowing person and the extent to which this person is indeed autonomous with respect to social influence and social control. As we shall try to show in the second half of this chapter, the self-knower school is singular in regarding self-knowledge as a liberating force, as an element that unleashes the person's potential autonomy, creativity, or spontaneity. Once we move to the more scientifically testable analysis of self-knowledge, as in self-cognizing, the relationship between autonomy and self-knowledge makes a radical shift.

The second issue, comprising the first half of the chapter, has to do with the person who knows, observes, or produces, in part, the self-knower. Here, we are referring, for example, to the parent, teacher, or acquaintance. We shall use the term *partner* to designate this person. Our question here is a simple one: Is the partner in the position to take heed of another's freedom and spontaneity, and of the other's unique, perhaps even objectionable, values? And how does the nature of the relationship between the partner and the potential self-knower affect our question? If the other is important to the partner, is the partner then more ready to appreciate and approve of the other's autonomy? Simplifying the issue somewhat, we would like to point the reader in the direction of the following problem: If a person (a potentially self-knowing person) demonstrates objective independence, refusal to be influenced, and the like, will the partner be able to accept this condition? Our overriding hypothesis, developed in part in Chapter 5, is that such objective autonomy will lead the partner to be unaccepting of that autonomy, and in turn, to ascribe less creativity, sensitivity, and self-knowledge to the other.

THE PARTNER: ORIENTED TOWARD STABILITY AND CONTROL

Not Wanting to Acknowledge the Other's Autonomy

If a partner is to appreciate another's self-knowledge, autonomy, flexibility, or readiness to be spontaneous, then that partner has to be open to those nonconstant features. Perhaps the most important prerequisite for a true appreciation of the free, autonomous other is that the other not be regarded as a static set of traits, nor as a unified system of behavioral dispositions. If a partner analyzes the other person in terms of "always gregarious," "invariably timid," "predictable," and the like, then the self-knower's capacity to be different, unique, changeable, and spontaneous, and to show a possibility of growth is not acknowledged. But what actually happens in person perception? There is, fortunately, a line of research that informs us quite directly about some differences between perceiving oneself and perceiving a partner. And in turn, this line of research implies that the partner is seldom in a position to be as open in perceiving the other as in perception of self. The differences are sometimes remarkable.

A direct example of such a process was first shown by Nisbett, Caputo, Legant, and Maracek (1973). The participants in one of their studies were given a task of depicting others along personality-item dimensions, such as "energetic-relaxed," and in addition, the subjects had to rate themselves as well. For each of the items, the subjects had the option of not indicating a score on the personality dimension and, instead, checking "depends on the situation." They were considerably more likely to check the "depends on the situation" alternative when rating themselves than when rating another person. This outcome led Nisbett *et al.*, in line with the thinking of Jones and Nisbett (1972), to conclude that the perception of others is often bound up with the ascribing of stable personality traits, whereas perception of oneself is more associated with situational influences and perhaps even with more change. This same effect has been demonstrated by other researchers (e.g., Funder, 1980; White & Younger, 1988). The point is that we, as observers, like to see others' traits or habits as remaining constant. This conclusion becomes even bolder in looking at an interesting effect reported by Sande, Goethals, and Radloff (1988). Their subjects simply filled out items such as the following:

To what extent would you describe yourself as:

a. serious

    not at all   very much

b. carefree

    not at all   very much   (p. 14)

As the reader will note, the participants had the possibility of assenting to mutually contradictory traits (e.g., serious and carefree). The subjects filled out the scales for themselves, and also from the perspective of an acquaintance. The findings were convincing evidence that we desire a relatively constant picture of others, in that the subjects were more apt to endorse mutually contradictory traits for themselves than for others. Translated a bit, this means that, in ourselves, we acknowledge the possibility of being serious *as well as* carefree, or perhaps kind as well as aggressive, but that we prefer to regard others as possessing a constant, internally consistent essence.

If we go back to the theme of the self-knower, the idea is that we, as partners, are not attracted by the possibility of another person's changing or performing mutually contradictory actions. The other's freedom of movement or freedom to change is not the partner's primary concern. We like to think that others have been the way they are for a long time, and that they are not about to change, regress, grow, or otherwise alter their characteristics. This applies to all of the desired characteristics that self-knowers are presumed to possess: freedom, spontaneity, creativity, warmth, and consistency. The partner who ascribes such qualities hopes that these may be regarded as part of an ongoing, durable package of behavior potentials.

THE OBSERVER AS REDUCTIONIST: NOT LOOKING AT THE PERSPECTIVE

Consider more carefully the psychology of the partner, the person who is asked to make judgments about another's autonomy, flexibility, and the like. The partner (i.e., perceiver of other persons) whom we see in studies such as those of Nisbett *et al.* (1973), Sande *et al.* (1988), or Funder (1980), performs self-observations in a manner quite different from the way in which others are observed. One's own actions are more likely to be regarded as owing to situational influences, whereas others' behaviors stem from unchanging dispositions or traits. Second, one's own actions or action tendencies are regarded as flexible, in the sense that people see their *own* potentials in terms of "friendly as well as unfriendly," "reliable as well as spontaneous." In contrast, other people are regarded in a much more one-sided manner, so that their behaviors or behavioral tendencies, across time, are described as constant.

What does this perception style mean in terms of causality? The other person's behavior is regarded as fixed. Relative to one's own past and future, that of the other person is seen as constant, as determined by fixed action tendencies. Compared to descriptions of one's own being, the partner does not tend to view others as spontaneous, flexible, or free.

While there have been different kinds of explanations of the partner's tendency to reduce the other person to a fixed trait portrait, the account that we focus on here relates to the partner's desire to have control over the other. A general principle stemming from attribution theory (Heider, 1958; Jones & Davis, 1965; Kelly, 1972) views much of person perception as being determined by the needs of the perceiver. If it can be assumed that the partner generally has some desire to predict or control the actions and thoughts of the other person, then we have the notion that a sense of predictability and control can be won by reducing the other to a fixed set of behavioral dispositions ("He always does that"; "He is always friendly"; "He seldom, if ever, helps").

The implication for our idealized self-knowledge analysis is unfavorable. If we want to assume that a certain individual has reached the ideal that is spelled out by the self-knower school (e.g., embodying autonomy, freedom from influence, and nonfacadelike behavior), we now have the problem of whether the partner will acknowledge the other's having reached self-knower status. Given that the characteristic partner has a desire to regard the other as a fixed entity, as unvarying, it seems that partners are more likely to perceive *themselves* as embodying self-knowing characteristics than to acknowledge the other as the embodiment of that idealized status.

IS THERE A BETTER-THAN-AVERAGE PARTNER?

The problems to which we have just alluded can be solved easily, at least on a practical level, if we can just locate those kinds of partners who show more openness or flexibility in perceiving other individuals. For instance, if we could find people who do not immediately reduce others to static bundles of fixed action tendencies, we would be on the right track. Funder (1980) provided a hint in this direction. Extrapolating from the Nisbett *et al.* (1973) procedure, he asked his respondents to fill out a list of 20 personality traits, rating (1) themselves, (2) a friend, and (3) a more distant acquaintance. As in the Nisbett *et al.* experiment, the subjects had the option for each trait rating of indicating "depends on the situation." If we take the quantity of "depends-on-the-situation" responses as a reflection of the subjects' sensitivity to possible variation in the other's behavior, we can begin to differentiate among the respondents in terms of such a sensitivity.

Funder had obtained information on the personality traits of his subjects (these were ratings by acquaintances of the subjects), and he found the following: The subjects who were most inclined to check "depends on the situation" were relatively free of anxiety, had a sense of humor, got along with others better, and generally created the image of a psychologically healthy, social, nonneurotic person. Accordingly, it looks as if one can locate certain individuals who are more capable of acknowledging the other's freedom and changeableness, and who are not so quick to ascribe permanent essences to the other. Unfortunately, this solution is only a superficial one, in that it does not address the nature of the "partnership" between the two parties (the potential self-knower and the partner). As soon as we delve into the course of this interaction we begin to see some further developments.

CONTROL DESIRES AND THE ASCRIPTION OF PERMANENCE

Once again, our question is: To what extent is the partner capable of acknowledging the other's autonomy or independence? This time, however, rather than posing the question in such a sweeping, nondifferentiated manner, we will look at how the nature of the partnership affects the ascriptions or judgments that the partner makes. In particular, we will focus on the extent to which the other poses a threat to the partner's control.

Another person, such as a potential partner, client, or experimental subject, can create a certain degree of uncertainty in the partner. An unfamiliar individual is likely to do the unexpected, make the partner uncomfortable, call for responses that are not available, and in general, bring the perceiver's control into question. A logical response to such a threat to control would be to rehearse one's own actions or to attempt to discover more about the other's background. But it is Miller and Norman's thesis (1975) that a certain shortcut is taken in reacting to the control-threatening person: the partner proceeds to try to render the person stable.

Obviously, the other cannot be transformed into a stable entity objectively; instead, the perceiver adopts the tack of trying to regard the individual as a stable entity. More concretely, in terms of the operationalizations of Miller and Norman (1975), Berscheid, et al. (1976), and Miller et al. (1978), this means trying to emphasize the person's long-term personality characteristics. Subjects threatened with control on the grounds of anticipated exchange with an unknown person are prone to be increasingly interested in the chronic behavioral dispositions of the new partner.

What does the experimental situation look like more concretely? Respondents (whom we will call *partners*) are placed in either of two circumstances. In one case, where there is little involvement with the other, they simply observe the other at a distance while the other is interacting (e.g., playing a game) with still another individual. The respondent (partner) expects no interaction with this other person. In a second case, the partner expects future interaction with the other, and following the assumptions of Miller and Norman (1975), this simple expectation should create a certain degree of uneasiness in the respondents. They do not know the person, they do not have a definite behavioral repertoire that can be applied to the setting, and thus their control is threatened. How weighty such a control threat is depends, of course, on such factors as the nature of the forthcoming interaction. In the Berscheid *et al.* (1976) paradigm, the interaction had the character of a quasi-date with someone of the opposite sex. We can presume that their subjects were highly ego-involved and uncertain about what would happen.

DOES INVOLVEMENT FACILITATE THE PERCEIVING OF OTHERS?

Miller and colleagues (1975, 1978) assessed their respondents' estimates of "how much they learned about the other's personality"; and Berscheid *et al.* (1976) measured the extremity of personality ratings ascribed by the respondent to the other. The findings of these several studies point unequivocally in the same direction: to the degree that an interaction was expected, there was a stronger urge in the direction of regarding the other as a stable entity, as a person who was unlikely to change. This finding conforms very nicely to the idea that threatened control in an interpersonal setting produces a readiness to define the other not as a flexible, changeable, spontaneous being, but as a fixed set of traitlike characteristics.

The implication for the central issue of this chapter is rather clear. Again, suppose that the partner is confronted with another who, in fact, behaves autonomously and so forth. To the extent that the partner must come to terms with that other behaviorally and thus actually interact with that other, objective autonomy or spontaneity is acknowledged to a lesser degree. And the more imposing the control threat, the greater is the reduction in the partner's ability or readiness to view another as a free, spontaneous, changeable entity.

THREAT TO CONTROL IN TERMS OF THE OTHER'S DISAGREEABILITY

The variation in control threat studied by Miller and Norman (1975) is only one route to defining the potential difficulties that a partner may have with the person being perceived. A further instance of control threat stems from settings in which the other insists on being disagreeable, cannot be influenced, espouses the "wrong" opinion, and the like. All such factors spell a difficult situation for the partner. One no longer knows exactly how the interaction will proceed, and to the degree that the partner's opinions or values are implicitly challenged, the exchange represents a loss of control for the partner.

We saw illustrations of this kind of situation in Chapter 5. In particular, a study by Eckert-Nowack (1988) created a substantial control threat to the partner, in that the other person (a younger student) did not accept the partner's advice regarding measures to be taken during the younger student's studies. The result of this control threat (i.e., the backfiring of the partner's influence attempt) was a derogation of the other. And most interesting for our present purposes was a reduction in *ascribed* self-knowledge: the young student who chose another path, who did not conform to the partner's suggestions, was subsequently regarded by the partner as relatively non-self-knowing.

We now have a partial answer to the issue of whether the partner is in the position of according another person autonomy, spontaneity, freedom, independence, and the like.

1. There is a general tendency to view the other in more static terms than those in which one views oneself. Characteristic partners ascribe more flexibility, changeability, and freedom to themselves than to another person.
2. As soon as the interaction becomes involving, the possibility of the partner's control needs comes to the fore, with the result that the other's actual flexibility is denied in favor of an image of the other that consists of fixed action tendencies. The perception of the other thus becomes rigid, evidencing a hope that the other will remain constant and predictable.
3. Perhaps most damaging to the idea that the partner can perceive the other's autonomy and freedom objectively is a very strong phenomenon: as soon as the other becomes disagreeable (i.e., objectively autonomous and not influenceable), the involved and influencing partner is inclined to ascribe *less* autonomy to the other, thus rejecting the other.

A CONCLUSION: THE INVOLVED PARTNER COMES TO EXACTLY THE WRONG INFERENCE

To conclude this section, we might look at an example in which two different children are central. One child has been raised so as to develop a definite, objective autonomy. She is slow to conform, feels free to disagree with others' opinions, and shows an objective independence in charting her course of behavior through various social situations. She does not copy the interests and hobbies of each child who comes along, and at the same time, she is likely to offer seemingly spontaneous suggestions for new directions or new solutions to problems. This is approximately the picture of the self-knower school's self-knower.

The second child is quite the opposite. He is highly sensitive to conformity pressures, is apt to emulate those around him, and seldom has anything ostensibly individual or unique to offer.

And now comes the partner: an adult who has to deal with each of these children for the first time. This could be a school counselor, a schoolteacher on the first day of school in September, or an estranged uncle or aunt who is encountering the child for the first time. Will this adult be in the position of acknowledging or appreciating the first child's autonomy and related qualities? We can now look at this problem in terms of the control threat posed for the adult, and in fact, we can examine two facets of this threat to control.

The first source of reduced control is the general uncertainty posed by a new person. The schoolteacher on the first day does not know exactly what to expect from, nor how to react to, the new pupil. Nor does the uncle or aunt know how the interaction will proceed, what the child will prefer to play with and so forth. Each of the children described above will threaten control in the sense of these uncertainties.

But there is a second source of control threat. The first child, the "self-knower"—the objectively autonomous, independent, individual child—will not readily abide by the teacher's, aunt's, or uncle's suggestions and philosophies. "Why should I do that?" is the likely reaction from the independent child. "Yes, I can see that" is the preferred reaction from the second, objectively *not* autonomous child. And what is the result of these first encounters? Everything we have discussed above points toward a conclusion that will now be all too obvious: The first child will be dealt with more as a set of static traits because the adult will be impelled to find structure, to render the child predictable and "understandable." And this same first child, the uncontrollable child, will be devalued and downgraded, and accompanying this evaluation will be a lesser ascription of self-knowledge, autonomy, maturity, and creativity. The adult thus commits a remarkable error of perception, labeling objective autonomy as nonautonomy, as non-self-knowingness. This completes our discussion of the partner—the adult, the teacher, the researcher, the therapist. We have no basis for saying that the characteristic partner is in a position to recognize or acknowledge actual autonomy; even worse, we have good reason to think that newness, control threat, and disagreeableness will lead the perceiver to exactly the wrong conclusion about which person has indeed achieved the traits that are supposed to be characteristic of the self-knower.

THE SELF-COGNIZING PERSON:
UNDER SOCIETAL CONTROL

ONE MORE GLANCE AT THE SELF-KNOWER SCHOOL: WHERE ARE THE REWARDS FOR SOCIETY?

The above discussion leads us to a paradoxical conclusion if we continue to abide by the definition of the self-knower as an autonomous individual. The more obedient, pleasant, and consistent a person is for a partner, the greater is the tendency of the partner to ascribe favorable qualities to that person, including such traits as creativity, intelligence, and even *self-knowledge*. Nowhere in any of the literature is there an indication that intense initial contact with a person produces a tendency in the partner to want the other to become more independent, autonomous, different, and the like. Thus, from a societal perspective, the ideal persons are those who let themselves be controlled by the partner, and this is particularly so when the other's behaviors have longer range or uncertain implications for the partner.

On the other hand, our previous chapters have adopted the point of view that a scientific analysis of self-knowledge requires the abandonment of the self-knower school, where the concept *self-knowledge* is equated with certain fixed characteristics. And in place of the self-knower school, we have looked at analyses that regard self-knowledge as being defined through cognitive contact with one's own behavior, and as self-cognizing in a broad sense. The question is now whether these other perspectives on self-knowledge tell us anything about freedom and autonomy. Does the cognizing of oneself—more particularly of one's behavioral potential—produce a sense of freedom, open up new behavioral options, or lead to a creative and autonomous person in any important sense? Let us have a direct look at the self-cognizing individual and try to determine whether the outcome is indeed autonomy, and then, in turn, one can ask what this outcome means for the partner and for the individual's society.

SELF-KNOWLEDGE AS COGNIZING ONE'S OWN BEHAVIOR

One scientific approach to self-knowledge is a model by Fazio and Zanna (1978; Fazio, 1986). The idea is simply that attitudes do indeed exist, as latent behavioral potentials, but that they have no particular psychological impact until they are rendered salient, that is, cognitively accessible. One sensible way of implementing this idea is to bring the behaviors that are basic to the attitudes into the picture. For instance, when respondents are asked about their attitudes toward a racial minority, they will of course answer with an "attitude," but according to the Fazio and Zanna argument, this attitude does not necessarily bear on behavior. In short, people giving an "attitude" statement are not always in the position of knowing themselves, in this case not knowing their own behavioral penchants. This kind of self-knowledge is a prerequisite for the attitude to be valid.

The cure, according to the Fazio and Zanna thinking, would entail letting the person interact with members of the racial minority before responding to the attitude measure. Only then is the behavioral basis of the attitude (i.e., the actual behavioral potential) likely to be salient and to exert its effects on the manner in which the attitude statements are given.

This simple procedure of bringing the person into direct contact with the behavioral tendency itself has two kinds of outcomes, as measured by Fazio and Zanna: (1) the person is capable of responding more quickly to the attitude measure, which is a sign of the person's having more immediate contact with the attitude, and (2) the person is subsequently more inclined to behave in a manner consistent with the attitude statement.

Although the Fazio and Zanna paradigms have been limited to attitudes, the idea can obviously be extended to almost any form of concrete behavioral potential, such as liberalism or extraversion. And regarded as a self-knowledge theory, it is straightforward in its implications: Self-descriptions concerning what one is likely to do in the future are valid only when the behavioral base of those self-descriptions is cognitively accessible.

The question now is whether this variety of self-knowledge brings with it an increase in autonomy, in any form whatever. The answer depends on whose perspective we assume in considering the problem. If the salience of past behavior increases the likelihood that *future* behavior will be in line with one's expressed attitudes, then there is ostensibly a gain in autonomy. That is, a behavior that is congruent with one's attitude is not necessarily going to be congruent with the dictates of current group pressures. Rather than succumb to concrete sources of social influence within a given situation, the person with self-knowledge as defined here will abide by previously stated attitudes. But there is an alternate perspective. If the attitude derives from habitual behavioral tendencies, then we need to ask where these tendencies came from.

If one's own group, parents, or teachers instill the behavioral tendencies in the first place, as well as the self-descriptions that accompany these tendencies, then we cannot very well speak of autonomy when we observe that a person shows an attitude–behavior consistency. Rather, this is exactly the consistency that the society tries to build into the individual. Following the Fazio and Zanna model, this consistency will not always occur; it is not automatic. Instead, certain procedures have to be undertaken to ensure that the behavioral tendency will be cognitively accessible or dominant, and once this is done, the previous influence of the person's society is once again felt.

The issue "autonomy or controllability?" thus depends largely on whose perspective we want to consider. The naive observer, not knowing anything about the individual's background, will greet an instance of attitude–behavior consistency as a sign of autonomy or independence. Consistent persons appear to defy current social pressures or at least to have their "own" sense of direction. The more naive the observer with respect to the other's background, the more impactful is the apparent autonomy. But if we know how the behavioral tendency and attitude were formed, and if we understand the process described by Fazio and Zanna, then we no longer see autonomy. Rather, self-knowledge (as cognizing one's past relevant behaviors) produces an adherence to the rules or teachings of one's background. The self-knowing person becomes a highly controllable entity.

SELF-KNOWLEDGE AS SELF-COGNIZING

The self-cognizing person shows a substantial increment in consistency between values and behavior or between personality and behavior, as illustrated in the previous chapter (Carver, 1975; Gibbons, 1978; Hormuth, 1982). An atmosphere that is conducive to self-reflexive attention brings the person to focus on pertinent standards, and the studies cited point to the role of self-focus in the person's abiding by culturally implanted values or personality dispositions.

Autonomy? Once again, we have to be rather naive observers to conclude that the self-knowing person (this time in the sense of simple self-cognizing) is "genuinely" autonomous. If we were willing to assume that people freely choose their values regarding punitiveness, sex, or whatever other issues, then the observed patterns all seem to fit the autonomy picture; that is, on the basis of a self-chosen value, the self-focused person behaves consistently with that value.

But let us move one step beyond this naïveté. Obviously, a person's punitiveness, creativity, or puritanism has roots in social influences. We do not need to belabor the point by citing learning theories or imitation theories. And if it is conceivable that a person's punitiveness or other value or disposition has roots in a certain group, it is a simple jump to the control notion that was explicit in the writings of Shibutani (1961): The simple inward-turning of one's attention may be seen as mediating and furthering the products of civilization. Many observers may not agree with the direction of that civilization (e.g., propunitive), but the agreeableness of the product to the observer does not alter the process. Once a value is implanted and exists as a latent behavioral potential, self-knowledge in the form of a simple self-cognizing induction brings that value into reality, onto a behavioral plane of functioning.

Of course, one cannot rule out the possibility of conflict among two or more values. In such cases, the relative salience of the competing values would seem to be the element that decides which of the values will come to predominate in behavior, as has been illustrated by Baldwin and Holmes (1987), Gibbons and Wright (1983), and Vallacher and Solodky (1979).

FURTHER SYMPTOMS OF SOCIETAL CONTROL

Numerous experimental studies have shown the impact of self-cognizing on the person's motivation to work harder and/or to abide more by widespread cultural standards (Carver & Scheier, 1981; Diener & Wallbom, 1976; Liebling & Shaver, 1973; Wicklund & Duval, 1971). But there are still other, qualitatively different indications of society's relatively iron hand over the self-knowing person. For example, confronted with negative outcomes for which one can take blame or not, self-focus is likely to result in ascription of responsibility to the self (Duval & Duval 1983; Duval & Wicklund, 1972, 1973; Mayer, Duval, Holtz, & Bowman, 1985). As another example, self-focus among people who are experiencing a particular deficiency has the effect of inducing self-criticism as measured by a fall in self-esteem (Brockner & Hulton, 1978; Ickes, Wicklund, & Ferris, 1973). As a third example, helplessness, or giving up in the face of adverse odds, is abetted by the induction of self-focused attention (Carver, Blaney & Scheier, 1979).

Accordingly, self-knowledge as a self-cognizing state appears thus far to be a valuable tool in a society that would like to control the individual. Certain values are implanted during socialization, the individual is brought into a self-cognizing state, and the result is a self-critical, self-blaming, highly consistent person who remains true to those values. Where is the freedom or autonomy?

AUTONOMY IN AN ASOCIAL REALM

All of our examples have dealt with actual behavioral potential. Behavioral potential has been the focus throughout this book, primarily because psychologists interested in the self talk almost exclusively about the implications of the self in behavior, and because the ramifications of these discussions for therapy are necessarily related to behavioral outcomes (see Chapter 1). Nonetheless, we can turn once again to the dividing up of the total self as depicted by James (1890) and can give some thought to whether self-knowledge, viewed here in terms of general self-cognizing, produces anything like autonomy in the *asocial* realm.

Our most accessible example in terms of the accomplished research is the perception of one's own physiological processes. Directly to the point is the research of Gibbons *et al.* (1979) and Gibbons and Gaeddert (1984), showing what happens when the ingestion of a placebo is accompanied by false information about its effects. Under normal conditions (i.e., when the subject is told that the "drug" will have certain physiological consequences), the person appears to be duped into reporting those consequences even though their actual occurrence should be impossible physiologically. (For instance, the ingestion of baking soda should not generate any noticeable physiological effects.)

However, these suggestion effects disappear in large part when subjects are placed experimentally in a self-cognizing state. Self-knowledge thus brings persons into closer connection with their actual physiological workings, or at least into awareness of the impact of an ostensible drug on their physiological functioning. Is this not autonomy, in the sense that self-knowledge (i.e., self-focus) prevents the person from being influenced and duped by experimental instructions? To be sure, this is a case in which self-cognizing does not appear to enhance social control. The only fair conclusion on the basis of these studies by Gibbons and colleagues is that self-focus does bring people to weigh the physiological evidence more heavily, and therefore to disregard another's suggestion about their physiological functioning.

This conclusion brings us full circle to the self-knower school once again, where the idea of knowing one's deep inner being is said to be the core of self-knowledge. However, there is a major difference between the physiological effects discussed here and the role of "looking to the core" in the self-knower school. The present example is limited simply to a heightened awareness of one's situation-specific arousal; there is no evidence that attunement to one's physiological reactions has any implications for a broader range of reactions or, for that matter, implications for behavioral potential in any form whatsoever. The issue is the same one that surfaced in Chapter 2, in the context of Schachter's (1964) and Zillmann's (1978) research on emotion. It was Schachter's observation that physiological arousal, or changes in arousal *per se*, do not impart direction to emotions. Rather, the type and direction of emotion must be given through external cues, often social cues, and without such cues the physiological change remains simply a physiological element, not imparting any particular direction. Thus, the primary lesson of the Gibbons *et al.* (1979) and Gibbons and Gaeddert (1984) findings is that self-cognizing attunes the person to the connection between a social suggestion about a drug's effects and actual physiological responding. But the result does not bear on any further behavior to be enacted, nor does it imply that the self-focused person is therefore more likely to behave more autonomously across all areas.

THE MOTIVATED PARTNER: IMPATIENT AND PRESENT-ORIENTED

The preceding discussion leads us to a conclusion about the degree of symbiosis between the self-cognizing person and the partner of that person. We have found that the self-cognizing person is a controllable entity, one whose values are built in through learning and imitation processes in combination with actions taken in the context of those values, and we have also found that the state of self-cognizing brings those implanted values to dominate the person's current behavioral direction. Through the influence of self-cognizing, there is less room available for other factors—no matter what they may be—to determine the person's actions in any given concrete setting. The person's history, in terms of internalized values, controls the behavioral direction. To what extent is this kind of controllability recognized or welcomed by the partner?

We may return to the case of the two children who are controllable in two different senses in order to get a handle on this issue: The one child is controllable in the immediate situation. This is the child who is ready to abide by the other's attitudes, wishes, or whims, the one whose behaviors are at best unreliably guided by values that were imparted earlier. Thus, for a partner who needs control over the other, the person who is readily adaptable to each situation is the ideal. Consistency is desired by the partner only insofar as the consistency is based on the partner's own values or wishes.

The other child is controllable in a much different sense. This is the one who has internalized ways of thinking and acting in earlier social settings and who now remains true to those internalized aspects. Although this child is officially promoted by educators and parents, such a child is unwelcome to the partner who has a strong control need.

The result is that we have a case of conflicting control mechanisms. The self-cognizing person is controlled by previously instilled values and tends to abide by them, and this remaining-consistent-with-one's-history may well be unattractive to any given partner. Nonetheless, the individual is indeed controlled, in a very objective sense, through previous internalization. The partner, however, is focused entirely on control-in-the-present and is hardly interested in the other's past, or in whether the other is remaining consistent with the past. Accordingly, we cannot readily speak of a happy symbiotic relationship between the self-cognizing person and the partner who is motivated to control, because the directions that result from these two orientations often clash with one another.

On the other hand, there are certain facets associated with self-cognizing individuals that make them particularly attractive to the observing, controlling partner. One of these is the self-doubt or self-criticism associated with self-cognizing. If a person is on uncertain ground, is inexperienced, has undergone failure experiences, or does not carry along a strongly internalized value system in some critical area, that person is then liable to self-criticism and is more susceptible to contemporary social influence (Brockner & Hulton, 1978; Ickes et al., 1973; Wicklund & Duval, 1971; Wicklund & Ickes, 1972). If the person's past has led the person onto uncertain ground within some given behavioral area, self-cognizing can easily give the partner the upper hand: the person will be prone to show more self-blame and reduced self-esteem and will be more open to conformity pressures.

In fact, a weak or shaky personal background is the ideal prerequisite for the display of the symptoms that are seen as so attractive by the self-knower school. Here we have the person who is self-critical, is ready to accept blame, and more important, is ready to adopt the "correct" ways of thinking, that is, the values of the partner. In the context of Chapter 5, this is the person whom the partner ultimately regards as mature, intelligent, and even autonomous. This is the person whom the controlling partner labels the "self-knower."

WHEN THE CONTROLLED PERSON FITS INTO THE PARTNER'S MOLD: WHICH MOLD?

Throughout these chapters we have referred to the self-knower school as demanding from the "self-knowing person" a certain set of qualities, qualities that serve as criteria by which the self-knower theorist decides that someone is self-knowing, such as being mature and empathic and having a sense of humor. Our overriding portrait has been that of a partner, in need of control, looking favorably at another person to the extent that the other embodies the characteristics that we have drawn from the self-knower school (Jourard, Maslow, and Rogers), from Kohlberg, from Warshaw and Davis, and from others. Their idealized portrait of the human is a homogeneous-appearing cluster of traits of human qualities that stem from "humanistic" thinking.

Nonetheless, a partner's desire to control someone does not have to mean that the control attempt involves persuading the individual to espouse or embody the above list of humanistic values. A counterexample can be drawn from the theoretical work and interview contents of Adorno *et al.* (1950). The prejudiced personality (or more extremely formulated, the fascist personality) is said to uphold a value system that is quite the opposite of humanism: the value of work and punishment, the necessity of making sharp and definite distinctions among people, the rejection of the outgroup, the rejection of psychological thinking, and the like. Should such a prejudiced individual be one's partner, then a person who also upholds such philosophies will, of course, be accorded greater virtue and will be seen as stronger, more correct, more normal, knowing what is right, and more autonomous.

Schweder (1983) related this point vividly in pointing to the possibility that the humanistic set of values, as represented by Rogers, Kohlberg, and others, is not necessarily the universally recognized set of absolutes:

> The dominant theme of Kohlberg's essay is that what is moral is not a matter of taste or opinion. Kohlberg abhors relativism. He shudders at the idea that the moral codes of man might be like the languages and foods of man; different but equal. (p. 105) . . . he holds out secular humanism, egalitarianism, and the Bill of Rights as rational ideals or objective endpoints for the evolution of moral ideas. (p. 104)

In principle, a theorist may begin with any set of values—authoritarian, laissez-faire, capitalistic, socialistic, technocratic—and build an ideal personal portrait on the basis of those values. In turn, the people who are then controllable, thus agreeable, are also pronounced to be healthy, self-knowing, strong, and "one of us." And no matter which set of value premises underlies such a self-knower school, our criticism would take the same direction: If a school of thought does little more than categorize on the basis of criteria of goodness and then control individuals in the sense of trying to push them to fit into that idealized picture, then the psychology of self-knowledge has been neglected. Psychological variables are no longer present, and the personal history of the person is not viewed as pertinent.

Our countersuggestion has been spelled out throughout the last four chapters and follows directly when one takes the initial, relatively simple step of separating the content of the self from the dimension of knowing the self. As soon as this is done, we are brought to think about the content of the self, about the many different directions it can take, and about the sources of these different directions of behavioral readiness. We are also brought to think about *knowing* of those elements as a separate dimension, one that has psychological determinants and one that can bring forth the varieties of internalized behavioral potential.

REFERENCES

Adler, A. (1912). *Über den nervösen Charakter: Grundzüge einer vergleichenden Individual-Psychologie und Psychotherapie.* Wiesbaden: Bergmann.

Adorno, T. W., Frenkel-Brunswik, E., Levinson, D. J., & Sanford, R. N. (1950). *The authoritarian personality.* New York: Harper & Row.

Allport, G. W. (1937). *Pattern and growth in personality.* London: Holt, Rinehart, & Winston.

Allport, G. W. (1942). *Persönlichkeit. Struktur, Entwicklung und Erfassung der menschlichen Eigenart.* Meisenheim: Hain.

Andersen, S. M. (1984). Self-knowledge and social inference: 2. The diagnosticity of cognitive/affective and behavioral data. *Journal of Personality and Social Psychology, 46,* 294-307.

Andersen, S. M., & Ross, L. (1984). Self-knowledge and social inference: 1. The impact of cognitive/affective and behavioral data. *Journal of Personality and Social Psychology, 46,* 280-293.

Archer, R. L., Hormuth, S. E., & Berg, J. H. (1982). Avoidance of self-disclosure: An experiment under conditions of self-awareness. *Personality and Social Psychology Bulletin, 8,* 122-128.

Aronson, E., & Carlsmith, J. M. (1963). Effect of severity of threat on the evaluation of forbidden behavior. *Journal of Abnormal and Social Psychology, 66,* 584-588.

Asch, S. E. (1952). *Social psychology.* New York: Prentice-Hall.

Assagioli, R. A. (1973). *The act of will.* New York: Viking.

Axsom, D., & Cooper, J. (1984). Reducing weight by reducing dissonance: The role of effort justification in inducing weight loss. In E. Aronson (Ed.), *Readings about the social animal* (4th ed.). New York: Freeman.

Bagozzi, R. P., Yi, Y., & Baumgartner, J. (1990). The level of effort required for behavior as a moderator of the attitude-behavior relation. *European Journal of Social Psychology, 20,* 45-59.

Baldwin, M. W., & Holmes, J. G. (1987). Salient private audiences and awareness of the self. *Journal of Personality and Social Psychology, 52,* 1087-1098.

Bandler, R. J., Madaras, G. R., & Bem, D. J. (1968). Self-observation as a source of pain perception. *Journal of Personality and Social Psychology, 9,* 205-209.

Bandura, A. (1965). Vicarious processes: A case of no-trial learning. In L. Berkowitz (Ed.), *Advances in experimental social psychology* (Vol. 2, pp. 1-55). New York: Academic Press.

Bandura, A. (1969a). *Principles of behavior modification.* New York: Holt, Rinehart & Winston.

151

Bandura, A. (1969b). Social-learning theory of identificatory processes. In D. A. Goslin (Ed.), *Handbook of socialization theory and research*. Chicago: Rand McNally.

Bandura, A., & Walters, R. H. (1963). *Social learning and personality development*. New York: Holt, Rinehart & Winston.

Baumeister, R. F. (1986). *Identity: Cultural change and the struggle for self*. New York: Oxford University Press.

Bem, D. J. (1965). An experimental analysis of self-persuasion. *Journal of Experimental Social Psychology, 1*, 199–218.

Bem, D. J. (1972). Self-perception theory. In L. Berkowitz (Ed.), *Advances in experimental social psychology* (Vol. 6, pp. 1–62). New York: Academic Press.

Bem, D. J., & McConnell, H. K. (1970). Testing the self-perception explanation of dissonance phenomena: On the salience of premanipulation attitudes. *Journal of Personality and Social Psychology, 14*, 23–31.

Benenson, J. F., & Dweck, C. S. (1986). The development of trait explanations and self-evaluation in the academic and social domains. *Child Development, 57*, 1179–1187.

Berkowitz, L., & Knurek, D. A. (1969). Label-mediated hostility generalization. *Journal of Personality and Social Psychology, 13*, 200–206.

Berscheid, E., Graziano, W., Monson, T., & Dermer, M. (1976). Outcome dependency: Attention, attribution, and attraction. *Journal of Personality and Social Psychology, 34*, 978–989.

Beutler, L. E. (1981). Convergence in counseling and psychotherapy: A current look. *Clinical Psychology Review, 1*, 79–101.

Beutler, L. E., Pollack, S., & Jobe, A. (1978). "Acceptance," values, the therapeutic change. *Journal of Counseling and Clinical Psychology, 46*, 198–199.

Bradburn, N. M., Rips, L. J., & Shevell, S. K. (1987). Answering autobiographical questions: The impact of memory and inference on surveys. *Science, 236*, 157–161.

Brehm, J. W., & Cohen, A. R. (1962). *Explorations in cognitive dissonance*. New York: Wiley.

Brockner, J., & Hulton, A. J. B. (1978). How to reverse the vicious cycle of low self-esteem: The importance of attentional focus. *Journal of Experimental Social Psychology, 14*, 564–578.

Bromley, D. B. (1977). *Personality description in ordinary language*. London: Wiley.

Brooks, L. (1974). Interactive effects of sex and status on self-disclosure. *Journal of Counseling Psychology, 21*, 469–474.

Buss, A. H. (1961). *The psychology of aggression*. New York: Wiley.

Buss, A. H., & Durkee, A. (1957). An inventory for assessing different kinds of hostility. *Journal of Consulting Psychology, 21*, 343–349.

Cantor, N., & Kihlstrom, J. F. (1987). *Personality and social intelligence*. Englewood Cliffs, NJ: Prentice-Hall.

Carkhuff, R. R., & Pierce, R. (1967). Differential effects of therapist race and social class upon patient depth of self-exploration in the initial clinical interview. *Journal of Consulting Psychology, 31*, 632–634.

Carver, C. S. (1975). Physical aggression as a function of objective self-awareness and attitudes toward punishment. *Journal of Experimental Social Psychology, 11*, 510–519.

Carver, C. S., Blaney, P. H., & Scheier, M. F. (1979). Focus of attention, chronic expectancy, and responses to a feared stimulus. *Journal of Personality and Social Psychology, 37*, 1186–1195.

Carver, C. S., & Scheier, M. F. (1978). Self-focusing effects of dispositional self-consciousness, mirror-presence, and audience presence. *Journal of Personality and Social Psychology, 36*, 324–332.

Chelune, G. J. (Ed.). (1979). *Self-disclosure: Origins, patterns, and implications of openness in interpersonal relationships*. San Francisco: Jossey-Bass.

Cialdini, R. B., & Mirels, H. L. (1976). Sense of personal control and attributions about yielding and resisting persuasion targets. *Journal of Personality and Social Psychology, 33,* 395–402.

Cooley, C. H. (1902). *Human nature and the social order.* New York: Scribner's.

Crampton, M. (1981). Psychosynthesis. In R. J. Corsini (Ed.), *Handbook of innovative psychotherapies* (pp. 709–723). New York: Wiley.

Cravens, R. W. (1975). The need for approval and the private versus public disclosure of self. *Journal of Personality, 43,* 503–514.

Crowne, D. P. (1979), *The experimental study of personality.* Hillsdale, NJ: Erlbaum.

Crowne, D. P., & Marlowe, D. (1960). A new scale of social desirability independent of psychopathology. *Journal of Consulting Psychology, 24,* 349–354.

Crowne, D. P., & Marlowe, D. (1964). *The approval motive: Studies in evaluative dependence.* New York: Wiley.

Davis, D., & Brock, T. C. (1975). Use of first-person pronouns as a function of increased objective self-awareness and performance feedback. *Journal of Experimental Social Psychology, 11,* 381–388.

Deci, E. L. (1975). *Intrinsic motivation.* New York: Plenum Press.

Deci, E. L., & Ryan, R. M. (1985). *Intrinsic motivation and self-determination.* New York: Plenum Press.

Diener, E. (1979). Deindividuation, self-awareness and disinhibition. *Journal of Personality and Social Psychology, 37,* 1160–1171.

Diener, E., & Wallbom, M. (1976). Effects of self-awareness on antinormative behavior. *Journal of Research in Personality, 10,* 107–111.

Doob, L. W. (1947). The behavior of attitudes. *Psychological Review, 54,* 135–146.

Durkheim, E. (1951). *Suicide.* New York: Free Press. (Originally published 1897)

Duval, S. (1976). Conformity on a visual task as a function of personal novelty on attitudinal dimensions and being reminded of the object status of self. *Journal of Experimental Social Psychology, 12,* 87–98.

Duval, S., & Duval, V. H. (1983). *Consistency and cognition: A theory of causal attribution.* Hillsdale, NJ: Erlbaum.

Duval, S., & Wicklund, R. A. (1972). *A theory of objective self-awareness.* New York: Academic Press.

Duval, S., & Wicklund, R. A. (1973). Effects of objective self-awareness on attribution of causality. *Journal of Experimental Social Psychology, 9,* 17–31.

Eckert, M. (1987). *The perception of another's self-knowledge following a conflict situation.* Unpublished manuscript, Universität Bielefeld.

Eckert-Nowack, M. (1988). *Selbstkenntnis: Etikett für die kontrollierbare Person?* (Self-knowledge: A label for the controllable person?) Unpublished doctoral dissertation, Universität Bielefeld.

Elias, N. (1969). *Über den Prozess der Zivilisation* (Bd. 2). Bern: Francke.

Fazio, R. H. (1986). How do attitudes guide behavior? In R. M. Sorrentino & E. T. Higgins (Eds.), *Handbook of motivation and cognition: Foundations of social behavior* (pp. 204–243). New York: Guilford Press.

Fazio, R. H., Effrein, E. A., & Falender, V. J. (1981). Self-perceptions following social interaction. *Journal of Personality and Social Psychology, 41,* 232–242.

Fazio, R. H., Herr, P. M., & Olney, T. (1984). Attitude accessibility following a self-perception process. *Journal of Personality and Social Psychology, 47,* 277–286.

Fazio, R. H., & Zanna, M. P. (1978). On the predictive validity of attitudes: The roles of direct experience and confidence. *Journal of Personality, 46,* 228–243.

Fazio, R. H., & Zanna, M. P. (1981). Direct experience and attitude-behavior consistency. In L. Berkowitz (Ed.), *Advances in experimental social psychology* (Vol. 14, pp. 161–202). New York: Academic Press.

Fenigstein, A., & Levine, M. P. (1984). Self-attention, concept activation and the causal self. *Journal of Experimental Social Psychology, 20,* 231–245.

Fenigstein, A., Scheier, M. F., & Buss, A. H. (1975). Public and private self-consciousness: Assessment and theory. *Journal of Consulting and Clinical Psychology, 43,* 522–527.

Festinger, L. (1950). Informal social communication. *Psychological Review, 57,* 271–282.

Festinger, L. (1954). A theory of social comparison processes. *Human Relations, 7,* 117–140.

Festinger, L. (1957). *A theory of cognitive dissonance.* Stanford, CA: Stanford University Press.

Festinger, L., & Carlsmith, J. M. (1959). Cognitive consequences of forced compliance. *Journal of Abnormal and Social Psychology, 58,* 203–210.

Forisha, B. L. (1981). Feminist psychotherapy II. In R. J. Corsini (Ed.), *Handbook of innovative psychotherapies* (pp. 315–332). New York: Wiley.

Fox, J., Knapp, R. R., & Michael, W. B. (1968). Assessment of self-actualization of psychiatric patients: Validity of the personal orientation inventory. *Educational and Psychological Measurement, 28,* 565–569.

Frank, J. D. (1959). The dynamics of the psychotherapeutic relationship. *Psychiatry, 22,* 17–39.

Frankel, A., & Snyder, M. L. (1978). Poor performance following unsolvable problems: Learned helplessness or egoism? *Journal of Personality and Social Psychology, 36,* 1415–1423.

Freedman, J. L. (1965). Long-term behavioral effects of cognitive dissonance. *Journal of Experimental Social Psychology, 1,* 145–155.

Freedman, J. L., & Fraser, S. C. (1966). Compliance without pressure: The foot-in-the-door technique. *Journal of Personality and Social Psychology, 4,* 195–202.

Funder, D. C. (1980). The "trait" of ascribing traits: Individual differences in the tendency to trait ascription. *Journal of Research in Personality, 14,* 376–385.

Gibbons, F. X. (1978). Sexual standards and reactions to pornography: Enhancing behavioral consistency through self-focused attention. *Journal of Personality and Social Psychology, 36,* 976–987.

Gibbons, F. X. (1983). Self attention and self-report: The "veridicality" hypothesis. *Journal of Personality, 51,* 517–554.

Gibbons, F. X. (1990). Self-attention and behavior: A review and theoretical update. In M. P. Zanna (Ed.), *Advances in experimental social psychology* (Vol. 23, pp. 249–303). New York: Academic Press.

Gibbons, F. X., Carver, C. S., Scheier, M. F., & Hormuth, S. E. (1979). Self-focused attention and the placebo effect: Fooling some of the people some of the time. *Journal of Experimental Social Psychology, 15,* 263–274.

Gibbons, F. X., & Gaeddert, W. P. (1984). Focus of attention and placebo utility. *Journal of Experimental and Social Psychology, 20,* 159–176.

Gibbons, F. X., & Wicklund, R. A. (1976). Selective exposure to self. *Journal of Research in Personality, 10,* 98–106.

Gibbons, F. X., & Wright, R. A. (1983). Self-focused attention and reactions to conflicting standards. *Journal of Research in Personality, 17,* 263–273.

Gollwitzer, P. M., & Wicklund, R. A. (1985). Self-symbolizing and the neglect of others' perspectives. *Journal of Personality and Social Psychology, 48,* 702–715.

Gollwitzer, P. M., Wicklund, R. A., & Hilton, J. L. (1982). Admission of failure and symbolic self-completion: Extending Lewinian theory. *Journal of Personality and Social Psychology, 43,* 358–371.

Greenberg, J., & Musham, C. (1981). Avoiding and seeking self-focused attention. *Journal of Research in Personality, 15,* 191–200.

Gur, R. C., & Sackeim, H. A. (1979). Self-deception: A concept in search of a phenomenon. *Journal of Personality and Social Psychology, 37,* 147–169.

Heider, F. (1958). *The psychology of interpersonal relations.* New York: Wiley.

Hoffman, M. L. (1977). Moral internalization: Current theory and research. In L. Berkowitz (Ed.), *Advances in experimental social psychology* (Vol. 10, pp. 85–133). New York: Academic Press.

Hoffmann-Graff, M. A. (1977). Interviewer use of positive and negative self-disclosure and interviewer-subject sex pairing. *Journal of Counseling Psychology, 24,* 184–190.

Hormuth, S. E. (1982). Self-awareness and drive-theory: Comparing internal standards and dominant responses. *European Journal of Social Psychology, 12,* 31–45.

Hurley, J. R., & Hurley, S. J. (1969). Toward authenticity in measuring self-disclosure. *Journal of Counseling Psychology, 16,* 271–274.

Ickes, W. J., Wicklund, R. A., & Ferris, C. B. (1973). Objective self-awareness and self-esteem. *Journal of Experimental Social Psychology, 9,* 202–219.

Insko, C. A., & Oakes, W. F. (1966). Awareness and the "conditioning" of attitudes. *Journal of Personality and Social Psychology, 4,* 487–496.

Jackson, D. N. (1967). *Personality research form manual.* Goshen, NY: Research Psychologists Press.

James, W. (1884). What is an emotion? *Mind, 4,* 188–205.

James, W. (1890). *Principles of psychology.* New York: Holt, Rinehart, & Winston.

Jones, E. E., & Archer, R. L. (1976). Are there special effects of personalistic self-disclosure? *Journal of Experimental Social Psychology, 12,* 180–193.

Jones, E. E., & Berglas, S. (1978). Control of attributions about the self through self-handicapping strategies: The appeal of alcohol and the role of underachievement. *Personality and Social Psychology Bulletin, 4,* 200–206.

Jones, E. E., & Davis, K. E. (1965). A theory of correspondent inferences: From acts to dispositions. In L. Berkowitz (Ed.), *Advances in experimental social psychology* (Vol. 2, pp. 219–266). New York: Academic Press.

Jones, E. E., & Nisbett, R. E. (1972). The actor and the observer: Divergent perceptions of the causes of behavior. In E. E. Jones, D. E. Kanouse, H. H. Kelley, R. E. Nisbett, S. Valins, & B. Weiner (Eds.), *Attribution: Perceiving the causes of behavior* (pp. 79–94). Morristown, NJ: General Learning Press.

Jones, E. E., Rhodewalt, F., Berglas, S., & Skelton, J. A. (1981). Effects of strategic self-presentation on subsequent self-esteem. *Journal of Personality and Social Psychology, 41,* 407–421.

Jourard, S. M. (1958). *Personal adjustment.* London: Macmillan.

Jourard, S. M. (1961). Self-disclosure patterns in British and American college females. *Journal of Social Psychology, 54,* 315–320.

Jourard, S. M. (1968). Healthy personality and self-disclosure. In C. Gordon & K. J. Gergen (Eds.), *The self in social interaction* (Vol. 1, pp. 423–434). New York: Wiley.

Jourard, S. M. (1971). *The transparent self.* New York: Van Nostrand.

Jourard, S. M., & Lasakow, P. (1958). Some factors in self-disclosure. *Journal of Abnormal and Social Psychology, 56,* 91–98.

Kelley, H. H. (1972). Attribution in social interaction. In E. E. Jones, D. E. Kanouse, H. H. Kelley, R. E. Nisbett, S. Valins, & B. Weiner (Eds.), *Attribution: Perceiving the causes of behavior* (pp. 1–26). Morristown, NJ: General Learning Press.

Kiesler, D. J., Mathieu, P. L., & Klein, M. H. (1964). Sampling from the recorded therapy interview: A comparative study of different segment lengths. *Journal of Consulting Psychology, 28,* 349–357.

Kihlstrom, J. F., & Cantor, N. (1984). Mental representations of the self. In L. Berkowitz (Ed.), *Advances in experimental social psychology* (Vol. 17). New York: Academic Press.

Knapp, R. R., Shostrom, E. L., & Knapp, L. (1978). Assessment of the actualizing person. In P. McReynolds (Ed.), *Advances in psychological assessment* (Vol. 4, pp. 103–139). San Francisco: Jossey-Bass.

Koffka, K. (1935). *Principles of Gestalt psychology.* New York: Harcourt, Brace, & World.

Kohlberg, L. (1980). Stages of moral development as a basis for moral education. In B. Munsey (Ed.), *Moral development, moral education, and Kohlberg* (pp. 15–98). Birmingham, AL: Religious Education Press.

Koller, M., & Wicklund, R. A. (1988). Press and task difficulty as determinants of preoccupation with person descriptors. *Journal of Experimental Social Psychology, 24,* 256–274.

Lange, C. G. (1885). *Om Sinsbevaegelser.* Copenhagen: Rasmussen.

Langer, E. J., & Abelson, R. P. (1974). A patient by any other name . . . : Clinical group differences in labeling bias. *Journal of Consulting and Clinical Psychology, 42,* 4–9.

Langston, R. D. (1973). Sex guilt and sex behavior in college students. *Journal of Personality Assessment, 37,* 467–472.

Lepper, M. R., Greene, D. T., & Nisbett, R. E. (1973). Undermining children's intrinsic interest with extrinsic reward: A test of the overjustification hypothesis. *Journal of Personality and Social Psychology, 28,* 129–137.

Liebling, B. A., & Shaver, P. (1973). Evaluation, self-awareness, and task-performance. *Journal of Experimental Social Psychology, 9,* 297–306.

Locksley, A., & Lenauer, M. (1981). Considerations for a theory of self-inference processes. In N. Cantor & J. F. Kihlstrom (Eds.), *Personality, cognition, and social interaction* (pp. 263–277). Hillsdale, NJ: Erlbaum.

Luborksy, L., Crits-Christoph, P., Mintz, J., & Auerbach, A. (1988). *Who will benefit from psychotherapy? Predicting therapeutic outcomes.* New York: Basic Books.

Markus, H. (1977). Self-schemata and processing information about the self. *Journal of Personality and Social Psychology, 35,* 63–78.

Markus, H. (1983). Self-knowledge: An expanded view. *Journal of Personality, 51,* 543–565.

Markus, H., & Sentis, K. (1982). The self in social information processing. In J. Suls (Ed.), *Psychological perspectives on the self* (Vol. 1, pp. 41–70). Hillsdale, NJ: Erlbaum.

Maslow, A. H. (1961). Peak-experience as acute identity-experiences. *American Journal of Psychoanalysis, 21,* 254–260.

Maslow, A. H. (1968). Peak-experiences as acute identity-experiences. In C. Gordon & K. J. Gergen (Eds.), *The self in social interaction* (Vol. 1, pp. 275–280). New York: Wiley.

Maslow, A. H. (1971). *The farther reaches of human nature.* New York: Viking.

Maslow, A. H. (1977). *Motivation und Persönlichkeit.* Olten: Walter-Verlag.

Mayer, F. S., Duval, S., Holtz, R., & Bowman, C. (1985). Self-focus, helping request salience, felt responsibility, and helping behavior. *Personality and Social Psychology Bulletin, 11,* 133–134.

McArthur, L. Z., & Post, D. L. (1977). Figural emphasis and person perception. *Journal of Experimental Social Psychology, 13,* 520–535.

McGuire, W. J., & McGuire, C. V. (1981). The spontaneous self-concept as affected by personal distinctiveness. In A. Norem-Hebeisen, M. D. Lynch, & K. Gergen (Eds.), *The self-concept.* New York: Ballinger.

McGuire, W. J., & McGuire, C. V. (1982). Significant others in self-space: Sex differences and developmental trends in the social self. In J. Suls (Ed.), *Psychological perspectives on the self* (Vol. 1, pp. 71–96). Hillsdale, NJ: Erlbaum.

McGuire, W. J., McGuire, C. V., Child, P., & Fujioka, T. (1978). Salience of ethnicity in the spontaneous self-concept as a function of one's ethnic distinctivensss in the social environment. *Journal of Personality and Social Psychology, 36,* 511–520.

McGuire, W. J., & Padawer-Singer, A. (1976). Trait salience in the spontaneous self-concept. *Journal of Personality and Social Psychology, 33,* 743–754.

Mead, G. H. (1934). *Mind, self, and society.* Chicago: University of Chicago Press.

Miller, D. T., & Norman, S. A. (1975). Actor-observer differences in perceptions of effective control. *Journal of Personality and Social Psychology, 31,* 503–515.

Miller, D. T., Norman, S. A., & Wright, E. (1978). Distortion in perception as a consequence of the need for effective control. *Journal of Personality and Social Psychology, 36,* 598–607.

Miller, J. G. (1984). Culture and the development of everyday social explanation. *Journal of Personality and Social Psychology, 46,* 961–978.

Mischel, W. (1968). *Personality and assessment.* New York: Wiley.

Mohr, D. M. (1978). Development of attributes of personal identity. *Developmental Psychology, 14,* 427–428.

Mosher, D. L. (1968). Measurement of guilt in females by self-report inventories. *Journal of Consulting and Clinical Psychology, 32,* 690–695.

Mowrer, O. H. (1964). *The new group therapy.* New York: Van Nostrand.

Nisbett, R. E., Caputo, C., Legant, P., & Maracek, J. (1973). Behavior as seen by the actor and as seen by the observer. *Journal of Personality and Social Psychology, 27,* 154–156.

Nisbett, R. E., & Wilson, T. D. (1977a). The halo effect: Evidence for unconscious alteration of judgments. *Journal of Personality and Social Psychology, 35,* 250–256.

Nisbett, R. E., & Wilson, T. D. (1977b). Telling more than we can know: Verbal reports on mental processes. *Psychological Review, 84,* 231–259.

Ortlieb, P. (1973). Sozialpsychologische Grundlagen psychotherapeutisch vermittelter "Einsicht." *Gruppendynamik, 3,* 202–212.

Palermo, D. S., & Jenkins, J. J. (1964). *Word association norms: Grade school through college.* Minneapolis: University of Minnesota Press.

Pepinsky, H. B., & Karst, T. O. (1964). Convergence: A phenomenon in counseling and in psychotherapy. *American Psychologist, 19,* 333–338.

Persons, R. W., & Pepinsky, H. B. (1966). Convergence in psychotherapy with delinquent boys. *Journal of Counseling Psychology, 13,* 329–334.

Powell, M. C., & Fazio, R. H. (1984). Attitude accessibility as a function of repeated attitudinal expression. *Personality and Social Psychology Bulletin, 10,* 139–148.

Pryor, J. B., Gibbons, F. X., Wicklund, R. A., Fazio, R. H., & Hood, R. (1977). Self-focused attention and self report validity. *Journal of Personality, 45,* 513–527.

Pyszczynski, T., Holt, J., & Greenberg, J. (1987). Depression, self-focused attention, and expectancies for positive and negative future life events for self and others. *Journal of Personality and Social Psychology, 52,* 994– 1001.

Regan, D. T., & Fazio, R. H. (1977). On the consistency between attitude and behavior: Look to the method of attitude formation. *Journal of Experimental Social Psychology, 13,* 38–45.

Reiser, B. J., Black, J. B., & Abelson, R. P. (1985). Knowledge structures in the organization and retrieval of autobiographical memories. *Cognitive Psychology, 17,* 89–137.

Rholes, W. S., & Ruble, D. N. (1984). Children's understanding of dispositional characteristics of others. *Child Development, 55,* 550–560.

Rogers, C. R. (1950). The significance of the self-regarding attitudes and perceptions. In M. L. Reymert (Ed.), *Feeling and emotion: The Mooseheart Symposium* (pp. 374–382). New York: McGraw-Hill.

Rogers, C. R. (1951). *Client-centered therapy.* Boston: Houghton Mifflin.

Rogers, C. R. (1961). *On becoming a person.* London: Constable & Company.

Rosenthal, D. (1955). Changes in some moral values following psychotherapy. *Journal of Consulting Psychology, 19,* 431–436.

Salovey, P., & Turk, D. C. (1991). Clinical judgment and decision making. In C. R. Snyder & D. R. Forsyth (Eds.), *Handbook of social and clinical psychology: The health perspective* (pp. 416–437). Elmsford, NY: Pergamon Press.

Sande, G. N., Goethals, G. R., & Radloff, C. E. (1988). Perceiving one's own traits and others': The multifaceted self. *Journal of Personality and Social Psychology, 54,* 13–20.

Schachter, S. (1964). The interaction of cognitive and physiological determinants of emotional state. In L. Berkowitz (Ed.), *Advances in experimental social psychology* (Vol. 1, pp. 49–80). New York: Academic Press.

Schachter, S., & Singer, J. E. (1962). Cognitive, social and physiological determinants of emotional state. *Psychological Review, 69,* 379–399.

Scheier, M. F., Buss, A. H., & Buss, D. M. (1978). Self-consciousness, self-report of aggressiveness and aggression. *Journal of Research in Personality, 12,* 133–140.

Scherwitz, L., Graham, L. E., & Ornish, D. (1985). Self-involvement and the risk factors for coronary heart disease. *Advances, Institute for the Advancement of Health, 2,* 6–18.

Schweder, R. (1983). Review of Lawrence Kohlberg's *Essays in Moral Development: Vol. 1. The Philosophy of Moral Development.* In J. A. Meacham (Ed.), *Contributions to human development* (pp. 104–109). Basel: S. Karger.

Scott, W. (1965). *Values and organizations: A study of fraternities and sororities.* Chicago: Rand McNally.

Sennett, R. (1974). *The fall of public man.* New York: Random House.

Sherif, M. (1936). *The psychology of social norms.* New York: Harper.

Shibutani, T. (1961). *Society and personality: An interactionist approach to social psychology.* Englewood Cliffs, NJ: Prentice-Hall.

Shostrom, E. L. (1963). *Personal orientation inventory.* San Diego: Edits.

Skinner, B. F. (1957).*Verbal behavior.* New York: Appleton-Century-Crofts.

Snyder, C. R. (1989). Reality negotiation: From excuses to hope and beyond. *Journal of Social and Clinical Psychology, 8,* 130–157.

Snyder, C. R. (1990). Self-handicapping processes and sequelae: On the taking of a psychological dive. In R. L. Higgins, C. R. Snyder, & S. Berglas (Eds.), *Self-handicapping: The paradox that isn't* (pp. 107–150). New York: Plenum Press.

Snyder, C. R., & Higgins, R. L. (1988). Excuses: Their effective role in the negotiation of reality. *Psychological Bulletin, 104,* 23–35.

Snyder, C. R., Irving, L. M., Sigmon, S., & Holleran, S. (1991). Reality negotiation and valence/linkage self theories: Psychic showdown at the "I'm OK" corral. In L. Montada, S.-H. Filipp, & M. Lerner (Eds.), *Crises and losses experiences in the adult years.* Hillsdale, NJ: Erlbaum.

Snyder, M. (1974). Self-monitoring of expressive behavior. *Journal of Personality and Social Psychology, 30,* 526–537.

Staats, A. W., & Staats, C. K. (1958). Attitudes established by classical conditioning. *Journal of Abnormal and Social Psychology, 57,* 37–40.

Stephenson, B., & Wicklund, R. A. (1983). Self-directed attention and taking the other's perspective. *Journal of Experimental Social Psychology, 19,* 58–77.

Strickland, B. R., & Crowne, D. P. (1963). Need for approval and the premature termination of psychotherapy. *Journal of Consulting Psychology, 27,* 95–101.

Swann, W. B. (1983). Self-verification: Bringing social reality into harmony with the self. In J. Suls & A. G. Greenwald (Eds.), *Psychological perspectives on the self* (Vol. 2, pp. 3–66). Hillsdale, NJ: Erlbaum.

Swann, W. B., Pelham, B. W., & Chidester, T. R. (1988). Change through paradox: Using self-verification to alter beliefs. *Journal of Personality and Social Psychology, 54*, 268–273.

Sweeney, P., & Moreland, R.L. (1980). *Self-schemas and the perserverance of beliefs about the self.* Paper presented at the annual meeting of the American Psychological Association, Montreal.

Temerlin, M. K. (1968). Suggestion effects in psychiatric diagnosis. *Journal of Nervous and Mental Disease, 147*, 349–353.

Thorndike, E. L. (1920). A constant error in psychological ratings. *Journal of Applied Psychology, 17*, 25–29.

Truax, C. B. (1966). Reinforcement and nonreinforcement in Rogerian Psychotherapy. *Journal of Abnormal Psychology, 71*, 1–9.

Vallacher, R. R., & Solodky, M. (1979). Objective self-awareness, standards of evaluation, and moral behavior. *Journal of Experimental Social Psychology, 15*, 254–262.

Verplanck, W. S. (1955). The control of the content of conversation: Reinforcement of statements of opinion. *Journal of Abnormal and Social Psychology, 51*, 668–676.

Walker, A., Rablen, R., & Rogers, C. R. (1960). Development of a scale to measure process changes in psychotherapy. *Journal of Clinical Psychology, 16*, 79–85.

Wallach, M. A., & Wallach, L. (1983). *Psychology's sanction for selfishness.* San Francisco: W. H. Freeman.

Warshaw, P. R., & Davis, F. D. (1984). Self-understanding and the accuracy of behavioral expectations. *Personality and Social Psychology Bulletin, 1*, 111–119.

Waterman, J. (1979). Family patterns of self-disclosure. In G. J. Chelune (Ed.), *Self-disclosure: Origins, patterns, and implications of openness in interpersonal relationships* (pp. 225–242). San Francisco: Jossey-Bass.

Weber, M. (1920). Die protestantische Ethik und der Geist des Kapitalismus. *Gesammelte Aufsätze zur Religionssoziologie, 1*, 17–206. Tübingen: Mohr.

Weisz, J., Balazs, L., & Adam, G. (1988). The influence of self-focused attention on heartbeat perception. *Psychophysiology, 25*, 193–199.

Wetzel, C. G., Wilson, T. D., & Kort, J. (1981). The halo-effect revisited: Forewarned is not forearmed. *Journal of Experimental Social Psychology, 17*, 427–439.

White, P.A., & Younger, D. P. (1988). Differences in the ascription of transient internal states to self and other. *Journal of Experimental Social Psychology, 24*, 292–309.

Wicker, A. W. (1969). Attitudes versus actions. The relationship of verbal and overt behavioral responses to attitude objects. *Journal of Social Issues, 25*, 41–78.

Wicklund, R. A. (1975). Objective self-awareness. In L. Berkowitz (Ed.), *Advances in experimental social psychology* (Vol. 8, pp. 233–275). New York: Academic Press.

Wicklund, R. A. (1982). Self-focused attention and the validity of self-reports. In M. P. Zanna, E. T. Higgins, & C. P. Herman (Eds.), *Consistency in social behavior: The Ontario Symposium* (Vol. 2, pp. 149–172). Hillsdale, NJ: Erlbaum.

Wicklund, R. A., & Braun, O. L. (1987). Incompetence and the concern with human categories. *Journal of Personality and Social Psychology, 53*, 373–382.

Wicklund, R. A., & Brehm, J. W. (1976). *Perspectives on cognitive dissonance.* Hillsdale: NJ: Erlbaum.

Wicklund, R. A., & Duval, S. (1971). Opinion change and performance facilitation as a result of objective self-awareness. *Journal of Experimental Social Psychology, 7*, 262–268.

Wicklund, R. A., & Eckert-Nowack, M. (1989). The ascription of self-knowledge as a halo-effect. *Basic and Applied Social Psychology, 10*, 355–370.

Wicklund, R. A., & Gollwitzer, P. M. (1981). Symbolic self-completion, attempted influence, and self-deprecation. *Basic and Applied Social Psychology, 2*, 89–114.

Wicklund, R. A., & Gollwitzer, P. M. (1982). *Symbolic self-completion*. Hillsdale, NJ: Erlbaum.
Wicklund, R. A., & Ickes, W. J. (1972). The effect of objective self-awareness on predecisional exposure to information. *Journal of Experimental Social Psychology, 8,* 378–387.
Willerman, L., Turner, R. G., & Peterson, M. (1976). A comparison of the predictive validity of typical and maximal personality measures. *Journal of Research in Personality, 10,* 482–492.
Wolff, W. (1932). Selbstbeurteilung und Fremdbeurteilung im wissentlichen und unwissentlichen Versuch. *Psychologische Forschung, 16,* 251–328.
Wortman, C. B., Adesman, P., Herman, E., & Greenberg, R. (1976). Self-disclosure: An attributional perspective. *Journal of Personality and Social Psychology, 33,* 184–191.
Wylie, R. C. (1974). *The self concept.* Lincoln: University of Nebraska Press.
Zanna, M. P., & Fazio, R. H. (1982). The attitude-behavior relation: Moving toward a third generation of research. In M. P. Zanna, E. T. Higgins, & C. P. Herman (Eds.), *Consistency in social behavior: The Ontario Symposium* (Vol. 2, pp. 283–301). Hillsdale, NJ: Erlbaum.
Zanna, M. P., Kiesler, C. A., & Pilkonis, P. A. (1970). Positive and negative affect established by classical conditioning. *Journal of Personality and Social Psychology, 14,* 321–328.
Zillmann, D. (1978). Attribution and misattribution of excitatory reactions. In J. H. Harvey, W. J. Ickes, & R. F. Kidd (Eds.), *New directions in attribution research* (Vol. 2, pp. 335–368). Hillsdale, NJ: Erlbaum.
Zurhorst, G. (1983). Wie "echt" können wir leben? *Psychologie Heute, 10,* 20–29.

AUTHOR INDEX

SUBJECT INDEX

Actual self, 36, 72
Altruism, 15
Attribution, 113–114, 136
Authoritarianism, 3, 26, 35, 149
Autonomy, 6, 10, 26–27, 29–30, 36–38, 58, 66, 68, 71, 77, 133–134, 136, 141–142, 144–146
  cluster, 68
Awareness, 5, 9, 29, 35, 47, 52, 80, 82, 91, 108–109, 111–113, 117, 119, 121, 131–132, 146

Behavioral disturbances, 3
Behavioral potential, 3–8, 36, 52–53, 76, 82, 84, 87–89, 91–92, 95, 97–98, 102, 105–106, 112, 116, 142–143, 146, 150
Behavioral tendency, 13, 38, 85, 106, 117, 136

Childhood experiences, 6, 8
Closeness, 59
Cognitive access, 6
Cognitive attunement, 5, 91
Compensation, 48–50, 53–54
Conformity pressure, 43, 148
Congeniality, 66, 69
Consistency, 30–31, 35, 37–38, 76, 114–115, 126, 133, 143
  index, 31
Control, 6, 8, 59, 62–63, 65, 69, 72–74, 108, 134, 136–138, 145–147, 149

Control (*cont.*)
  loss of, 70
  maintenance of, 70
  need, 57, 63, 71, 73–74, 77, 133, 147–148
  societal, 8, 36, 80, 105, 132, 142, 145
  threat, 138–139, 141
Convergence, 60–62
Creativity, 5, 38–39, 46, 124

Depression, 58, 129
Discrimination, 13
Dissonance theory, 103–104, 120
Distinctiveness, 79–80, 82

Egoism, 107–108, 111
Emotion, 11, 35, 83–84
Emotional label, 12
Emotional security, 19
Emotional states, 12
Extraversion, 99, 102, 105, 143

Feminist therapy, 29, 37

Gestalt psychology, 80, 82, 113

Halo effect, 66, 68

Identity, 1, 28–29
Imitation, 12–13
Inner condition, 42–43, 51
Inner psychological mechanism, 2

165